Star in the Hoosier Sky

Lawrence S. "Bo" Connor

Hawthorne Publishing
Carmel, IN 46033

ISBN: 0-9726273-6-7 (Softbound)

ISBN: 0-9726273-7-5 (Hardbound)

Visit our website: www.hawthornepub.com
to see more interesting books

Hawthorne Publishing
15601 Oak Road
Carmel, Indiana 46033
(317) 867-5183

In gratitude for their forbearance, this book is dedicated to Patty and our children, Carrie, Julie, Larry, Maureen, Janet and Michael, and their spouses Bill, Chris, Tom, Will and Joanna.

TABLE OF CONTENTS

Acknowledgments

I wish to thank the following persons for their assistance in writing this book: Edward H. Frank, R. Joseph Gelarden, Max Friedersdorf, Richard R. Roberts, Richard E. Cady, R. K. Shull, Myrta Pulliam, Jerry Clark, John H. Lyst, James D. Mitchell, Joseph Hallinan, Susan Headden, James Young, Carolyn Lautner, Gloria Keating, Donna Mullinix, Lee Giles, Forest Bowman, Leroy K. New, Carl Henn, Frank Fisse, Mac Trusnik , Becky Walter, Tridi Poston and especially for my wife, Patty, and daughter, Carrie Weigel.

Special appreciation to *The Indianapolis Star*

which granted persmission to use its archival photos and articles.

1 • The Way It Was

If a movie producer had wanted to film yet another remake of *The Front Page* the city room of *The Indianapolis Star* in the 1950s would have been an ideal setting. The place was crowded, noisy, and dingy. Cigarette butts and copy paper littered the linoleum-covered floor. Editors yelled at copy boys. Teletype machines hummed while turning out copy from the wire services, and reporters pounded out stories on Royal typewriters. Just about everyone smoked. By six o'clock when the staff was working on the first (or bulldog) edition, a haze hung over the newsroom.

There was always a shortage of desks, so most of the young reporters shared them. They were wooden with typewriter wells sunk in the middle, all of them scarred with cigarette burns. We were instructed to close up the desks at the end of each day, but few of us bothered. Desks were piled with notes, press releases, magazines, stacks of copy paper and half-filled paper coffee cups. Periodically the managing editor would issue an order to clean off the desktops. Two days later the piles returned.

I became part of that raucous newsroom in November of 1949. It was a place I had wanted to be since I was a boy. The meager pay ($42.50 a week) didn't dampen my enthusiasm, at least at that time. As a kid I loved movies about newspapers, getting a thrill out of watching Joel McCrea break the big story in *Foreign Correspondent*, and watching the wily managing editor, Walter Burns, manipulate ace reporter Hildy Johnson in *The Front Page*. I even liked the B-movies where brash reporters sported press passes in their hatbands.

I grew up in Hampton Court, an apartment complex a mile and a half north of *The Star* building. In the summer of 1937 several of the youngsters living in the apartments published three issues of a newspaper we first called the "Hampton Sentinel" and then switched to "The Court Reporter." It carried items about what was happening in the court. I loved looking at the paper after my dad had it printed where he worked.

But I didn't seriously consider journalism when I returned from three years in the Army Air Corps. Before I headed off to the University of Notre Dame, thanks to the G I Bill, I received some valuable advice from an uncle. I told him I thought I should take courses that promised better pay, mentioning that hotel and restaurant management was being touted as a lucrative field. He nixed that idea. He said that he traveled a lot and observed that hotel managers were faced with crises almost daily. Asked what I wanted to do, I told him I'd like to work on a newspaper but heard that the pay was meager.

"Do what you like," he said. "Don't worry about the money. You'll make a decent living," adding, "I've been an accountant all my life and hated every minute of it." So I took his advice and majored in journalism, though in the mid-1940s it had a grander title —communication arts.

I felt fortunate to be hired because so many ex-servicemen had been returning to the paper. The fact that my mother had worked with the paper's editor, Jim Stuart, in the first decade of the century probably helped in my being hired. There were no writing or reporting tests. It all depended upon whether there was an opening on the staff and the city editor thought you had possibilities.

It was all true about the lousy hours and the poor pay, but that didn't matter. I was just happy to have joined an assortment of colorful, irreverent and talented men and women in a profession that to me held the promise of excitement nearly every day.

When I was hired, *The Star* wasn't much of a newspaper, but most of the other medium-sized papers didn't have much going for them either. On most days *The Star* ran 24 to 28 pages split into two sections. Any advertising was inside the paper; the colorful inserts on slick paper arrived years later.

Like the rest of the city, the paper was recovering from the Depression and World War II. Throughout the war years, the paper printed an abundance of wire copy, mostly war news. The staff operated with a few decent reporters and a support crew of aged and uninspired reporters and copy editors, many with alcohol problems. Few of the older breed had college degrees. But many of them helped me learn the business both on the job and at bars and all-night eateries after we had left the building for the night.

The half dozen women who comprised the society department spent their time typing up wedding announcements and listing social events. Fashions and home furnishings stories went in the Sunday paper.

Corbin Patrick, who chronicled and promoted the city's cultural growth for more than 60 years, reported the city's meager arts and cultural scene. He joined the paper in 1925 and was named drama critic in 1941. He estimated that he reviewed 5,000 plays. Pat managed to find something redeeming in every show, especially local amateur productions. He was instrumental in gaining support for a symphony orchestra, the Ensemble Music Society and Clowes Hall. He was still interested in what was going

on at the paper and in the entertainment scene until he
2002.

Television became part of his bailiwick, but only after the publis
to acknowledge that ignoring TV wasn't working. Eventually, Cor
was able to hire an assistant and a woman to prepare the television grids. By then *TV Guide* was becoming the largest selling magazine in the U. S. The paper's art columnist, Lucille Morehouse, wrote her Sunday column in her Irvington home. A couple of times I was sent to her house to pick up her copy. Either her house lacked electricity, or she shunned it, because the rooms were illuminated with candles.

Gordon Milne was the garden editor. He spent most of his time answering calls from readers about the best times to plant petunias and how best to get a healthy lawn. Gordon was resourceful. He kept his Sunday columns in a file cabinet by his desk. When it was time to write the column, he would extract last year's column from the cabinet, mark it up and send it to the composing room. Why not, he reasoned; the advice from year to year was always the same. Gordon was the closest thing to a specialist on the staff.

The paper concentrated on politics, government and police news. Little attention was paid to education, religion and medical matters. If there was an Indianapolis School Board meeting that night, the city editor would look around for whoever might be available to cover it. The church editor confined her efforts to gathering short items about Sunday services. They covered the top half of the Saturday church page; the bottom half was devoted to ads about churches and ministers.

The editorial page was rigidly conservative. Most of the newsroom staff dismissed it as irrelevant; even contending that the best way for a candidate to get elected was to have his opponent indorsed by the paper.

Joe Cravens was the paper's sole photographer during most of the prewar years. He had photographed almost every Hoosier of note and every 500-Mile Race winner since the first one in 1911 until he retired in 1953. During the 1950s we operated with only four or five photographers, each equipped with the cumbersome Speed Graphic cameras. For years the photographers—"hypo sniffers"—were merely tolerated when they weren't being berated by editors. It was years before they were appreciated.

One of them, Dale Shofner, arrived early to record a luncheon at the governor's mansion. While awaiting arrival of the guests, the governor's wife, Mrs. Henry F. Schricker, invited Dale to sample the tray of hors d'ouevres. Dale, a tall, stout fellow, accepted the invitation and plucked half of the delicacies before the guests arrived. Mrs. Schricker, an otherwise gentle woman, complained to the society editor.

Bob Kellum, who lit each cigarette with the butt of the one he had been smoking, was our one-man business staff. Bob wrote a daily column, mostly a series of short items gleaned from press releases that came across his desk. He had an assistant handling the stock market listings. When I left the paper in 1990 the business staff had grown to 10 reporters and editors.

Kellum's successors included Don G. Campbell, an outstanding writer who wrote books on the stock market and real estate subjects, and James A. C. Thom, who became a successful writer of novels and non-fiction works about America in the 18th and 19th centuries. Jim had the rare ability to interview a person without taking notes. He would return to the office and turn out a column that included direct quotes of the person interviewed. He said he didn't need to take notes, that he remembered everything worth remembering. I never received a single complaint from anyone about being misquoted.

Gentle Charley Walker was the state editor. He kept in touch with about 100 correspondents in all of the counties. There was probably no one who knew more about Indiana than Charley. Frail and hunchbacked, he sat at his desk quietly taking information from the correspondents and churning out dozens of stories each day.

Mary Bostwick, a relic who was hanging on, jealously guarded her desk in a corner of the newsroom. That was one desk that wasn't shared with the staff. She had made a reputation as a stunt reporter when she joined *The Star* in 1913, driving around the Speedway track, soaring in a balloon race, and dangling from a rope high over a downtown intersection as part of a rescue operation by the fire department. But in the fifties she was just a cranky old woman who kept a loaded pistol in her desk, a souvenir from a trial in Colorado. The firing pin was shaved off. I think she wrote an occasional column for the editorial page. Mary was one of the few females on the staff. Today more than half of the staff is female and many of the editors are women. There were no blacks on the staff then.

Helen Connor, a thin, quiet, soft spoken woman helped to train hundreds of reporters and copy editors in her 38 years at the paper. She maintained the highest standards and was unfailingly patient with young reporters; working quietly with them to show how they could improve their reporting and writing. She ignored loud and profane outbursts in the newsroom and I can't ever remember hearing her even say "damn" or "hell." She acted as a buffer between the staff and the always demanding managing editor, Bob Early. When the staff threw a birthday party for her three years before she retired in 1982 some 200 people showed up at the Indianapolis Press Club. Former reporters and editors came from all parts of the country and one even flew in from Mexico City.

The Sunday editor, Julian Sullivan, was a mild young man who got into a heated argument with his wife one morning. Julian, the story goes, handed his wife a butcher knife after she said she'd like to kill him. "Go ahead," he said. And she did.

Al G. McCord was another of those valuable deskmen who seemed to know something about every person of note in the state. Quiet by nature, he'd erupt by slamming the receiver into the phone cradle after tolerating a troublesome caller. Al gave us some anxious moments when he'd light his pipe and toss the match into a large waste container by the city desk. More than once someone would have to grab a fire extinguisher to douse a fire in the container.

The sports staff in the fifties numbered a half dozen. They concentrated on high school sports, Indiana, Purdue and Butler, the Indianapolis Indians baseball team, and 500-Mile Race activity throughout the month of May. The sports department—sequestered in its own room—seemed to operate apart from the rest of the staff. Booze tended to infect the staff.

The entire staff was thin, but then it was always thin. In those first few years, the copy desk was manned by aged males who had put out the paper during the war. Most of them had run out of what little enthusiasm they had once had for the work.

Ben Cole, who was the paper's Washington correspondent for more than three decades, recalled those early years in a letter he wrote to me after retiring.

> I came to *The Star* from Terre Haute in March of 1944. I was about as welcome as a genealogist at a bastards' reunion. The copy desk was populated by some of the most dyspeptic and disgruntled human beings I had ever encountered. I had no

> previous experience with copy readers, hence did not know that dyspepsia and disgruntlement are congenital characteristics of the breed.

Charley Temple had moved from the copy desk to become news editor, but he retained his copy desk demeanor. His response to any query about "what's going on" never varied. It was always, "same old shit."

John Henry Johnson, a rail-thin, 6-foot, 6-inch copy editor and weekend news editor, said little to co-workers. He would arrive on the evening before his days off with an armload of library books. On his days off he and his wife (also an avid reader) would spend the weekend drinking whiskey, smoking cigarettes and reading books. His wife, wearing a diaphanous gown, was killed when she backed into a heater and the gown caught fire. John Henry died, a victim of alcohol.

Ovid Lane, an elderly copy editor, seldom spoke to any of us, but he did ask me one night if I would accept a date with his daughter. I lied my way out of it. It was Ovid who wrote the headline, "Record Crowd Sees Ball Game," on a page one short about the Yankees winning the fifth game of the World Series.

Joe Shepard, who ended up on the copy desk after a long career as a reporter and writer, principally on the *Star Magazine*, brought his wife's ashes in an urn and placed them on the desk in front of him.

And there was Ross Nelson, another relic from the war years, who became the telegraph editor. His job was to look over all of the copy that poured in continuously from the wire services on the teletype machines. He would use a scissors to select the stories he considered newsworthy enough to pass on to the news editor who arrived at 5 o'clock. But one afternoon Ross showed up after a stop at a tavern and decided to forgo making selections. Instead he took the continuous strips of copy from the wire machines, rolled them up in a neat package and handed it to the news editor with the comment, "Here it is, all wrapped up for you." Then he left for the day.

Few of those aged copy editors were enamored with their jobs. Lou Sullivan underwent a routine hernia operation and was off work six weeks recuperating. The day he returned to work, he told me he had three weeks vacation time accrued and went back home.

Leland Deckard was the grumpy news editor when I first joined the paper. His wife, Lee, ran the morgue (library) as though it was her private fiefdom.

Our longtime photo editor was Don McClure. His job was to select staff and wire photos to illustrate stories, and put together a half-page of pictures that ran on the bottom half of the back page of the daily paper. He had little control of the photographers; that was the job of the chief photographer, who assigned the photographers to carry out assignments made by the various desks. Don had been with the paper, along with his dour brother, Bill McClure, for many years. He was a happy sort, fueled occasionally by a trip to the clothes rack in the corner where he kept a half-pint bottle of gin in his overcoat pocket.

Bill McClure secluded himself in a corner of the newsroom where he handled the comics and syndicated features. He didn't mingle with the staff; still angry, I was told, about being passed over for the managing editor job that went to Bob Early a dozen years earlier.

Alcohol was a curse in many newsrooms and *The Star's* was no exception. One veteran general assignment reporter consumed 21 martinis one day at the Press Club, beginning with his first at 11 a. m. and winding up at midnight. Or so reported the club's bartender, Louis Cooper.

One night Dick Lennis noticed that the guy was holding an ashtray against his ear. "Ed, you're not going to get an answer that way." But Ed shot back, "I'm calling my wife."

Ed always insisted that he didn't have a drinking problem. I arrived in the city room one morning and found him on the floor wedged between the toilet stool and the wall in the men's room. He'd been there all night. He was one of the few staffers we fired, a step the paper rarely took.

Bob Mooney was one of the few reporters who whipped his alcoholism. He had help from a friend, Municipal Judge John Christ, who jailed him on some pretense and saw that he was placed in a padded cell. He battled the DTs in that cell and after treatment he returned to work and stayed sober for the rest of his life. Mooney loved being a political reporter and he knew just about every politician of any note in the state. He died at the young age of 57 following surgery. When cleaning out his desk that was piled high with press releases, clippings, notes and magazines, we discovered several uncashed payroll checks in one of the drawers.

Bob Hanika was another staffer who whipped the curse. He claimed that when he read in the paper that an 18-year-old girl's nearly nude body was found stuffed in a dresser drawer in the old Claypool Hotel, he panicked. He was recovering from a hangover but could not remember where he had been or what he had done over the weekend. "Oh my god, did I do it?" he wondered.

The girl, Dorothy Poore, a recent Clinton High School graduate, had come to the big city in hopes of finding a job. Police believe she was lured to the hotel room on the promise of a job and was suffocated with a pillow and her body placed in the drawer. Assistant managing editor Charles G. Griffo helped solve the crime. He noticed that the killer had registered at the Claypool as Jack O'Shea, and assumed it was an alias. Thinking that the man may have registered at another hotel, he discovered the man's real name by comparing his handwriting with the handwriting of a man named Victor Hale Lively who had registered at the Kirkwood Hotel. He had given a fictitious New York City address only slightly different from the one he had used at the Claypool. He was arrested in St. Louis, brought to trial and given a life sentence. "Griff's" sleuthing brought him a Pall Mall award.

I once asked Hanika if he ever missed alcohol.

"Only about every 15 minutes," he said.

There were several grungy taverns in the neighborhood and some are still operating. Because it was across New York Street from the paper, Markle's Tavern got a lot of late-night business from the staff. Few of us bothered to eat there, though. One early morning after work I spotted a two-foot long rat leaping along the food line. Our choice of restaurants at night was limited. There were two Chinese restaurants, one just north of the building and the other south across New York Street. Staffers heading out for dinner would leave word that they were going to "North Korea" or "South Korea." The St. Moritz was a favorite. If we were in a rush, there was always the greasy spoon restaurant in the alley behind the paper.

We got our first computers in 1974. It was called the Hendricks System. Half of the city room was torn up while a long table was installed holding a half dozen of the computers. Reporters lined up to take turns typing their stories on them. Now and then a story would disappear and we'd hear howls and cursing echo through the newsroom.

In another part of the building, 13 huge mainframe computers were installed in a temperature-controlled room. Four of them held the input from the classified advertising department, which operated on a different system. They are all gone now. One PC can hold as much information as all of them held then. Five years later the Hendrick's system was scrapped and replaced by a superior system.

The computers cut down on the noise from typewriters but the newsroom always looked like a teenager's bedroom.

Over the years improvements were made periodically. Today, with carpeting and silent computers operating in walled-off cubicles, the place is as quiet as a mortuary at 6 in the morning. But the desks are still piled high with newspapers, magazines, press releases, and whatever personal items land there.

One item still around was an open wooden coffin built by the carpenters for a story on how to dress a body for a funeral. Myrta Pulliam turned the coffin upright, installed some hooks in it, placed it next to the city desk, and used it as a coat rack. With each move she has made in the building, the coffin has gone with her and even today it rests in her office.

¤

2 •A Crusading Publisher

Eugene Collins Pulliam was one of the last of the crusading publishers who used their newspapers to hammer readers with their views on page one—and on the editorial pages. He had bought *The Star* in 1944—five years before I was hired.

He wore his hair in a crew cut, smoked dollar cigars, talked tough, and was a demanding, hard driving boss, a man of intense energy, a man who thrived on controversy, a man with a first-class ego. If one of his orders didn't get carried out, word came down from his sixth floor office that "heads will roll" but I never saw any heads rolling, including my own. In 41 years at the paper I never once saw him in the newsroom, and only one time in the building when I was sent to his office to deliver a package. As I stood in front of his desk, he never looked up from whatever he was studying. I laid the package on his desk and left.

Eugene C. Pulliam

He was a paternalistic publisher. Pay scales went up every year. The papers provided pension and health plans, and each Christmas and summer we all got bonuses. To Gene we were always the "Star-News family." He opened a recreation area for employees, and he set up a college scholarship program for children of workers.

He was 55 when he bought *The Star*. Reporters working then said the paper quickly changed, became livelier. He added women's pages and a Sunday magazine, beefed up the sports department, added columns to the editorial page, and ordered more coverage of the state. He got rid of sacred cows, though we picked up a few new untouchables over the years. He bought *The Indianapolis News* in 1948.

For the next three decades, *The Star* reflected his conservative views almost to the year he died at age 86 in 1975. I wonder if he ever had second thoughts about some of the orders he issued to carry out his conservative views. He wrote and talked about lofty journalistic principles but he managed to forget them when they interfered with a political goal.

He periodically called the newsroom around 7 o'clock in the evening when we were putting together the bulldog edition. Whoever answered the phone was given the order to put a story on page one blasting some politician in disfavor. Sometimes a copy boy would answer the phone and pass on the directive to an editor who was baffled about how to carry it out. The calls often came after a couple of scotches.

When John F. Kennedy was running for president in 1960 Pulliam wrote a page one editorial that he titled "You Can't Buy the White House." It backfired on him and on the paper. Despite the headline, the editorial didn't mention anything about buying the White House, but it charged Kennedy with "using his Catholic religion to attract sympathy." Pulliam was surprised when readers saw it as anti-Catholic.

In his biography of Pulliam his grandson, Russell Pulliam, related that shortly after the inauguration, Pulliam was seated next to Kennedy at a White House luncheon. "Kennedy told him that the editorial, 'You Can't Buy the White House' was one of the roughest he encountered in the campaign." Russ said his grandfather could only shrug his shoulders, but Kennedy added with a smile, "I did, didn't I?" That may have been the moment when Pulliam decided Kennedy wasn't a bad sort.

It was a different story with Bobby Kennedy, whom Pulliam detested.

Bobby was seeking the nomination for president in 1968 and we received a memo from ECP in Phoenix that read: "I think whenever Senator McCarthy [Eugene] comes to Indiana that we should give him as full coverage as possible—but this does not apply to a man named Kennedy." Throughout the campaign *The Star* assailed Bobby regularly in editorials and cartoons.

Pulliam's dislike of Bobby caused the paper acute embarrassment. It happened the night Reverend Martin Luther King, Jr. was assassinated in 1968 in Memphis. Pulliam called the newsroom to say that King was nothing but a "rabble-rouser" and ordered the story about his death played below the fold on page one. His son Gene, the associate publisher, overruled him and the story got major play. But that evening Bobby was in the city to give a campaign speech to a largely black audience at a neighborhood park at 1700 Broadway. Advisers urged him to cancel his appearance, but Kennedy went ahead and delivered what became a famous talk. It took courage to face the angry crowd but his remarks quieted them.

ECP later called with instructions to play down Kennedy's talk. And while the talk was making page one in papers across the country, we buried it in a story about favorite son Governor Roger Branigin receiving endorsements from student leaders in his futile quest for Indiana's votes for the nomination.

The treatment that Kennedy received throughout the campaign led him to complain that *The Star* was the worst paper in the United States, even worse than the notorious *Manchester Union-Leader*. Subsequently the *Co-*

lumbia Journalism Review savaged the paper in a long article about our biased coverage. The article concluded:

> When the line between a newspaper's editorial point of view and its reportage of the news becomes so blurred that the average reader no longer can be expected reasonably to discern where fact ends and opinion and propaganda take over, the community—and the integrity of the news business—are ill served.

Later in the fall, Pulliam reluctantly conceded to the paper's executives that "I guess we did go a little too far."

He went a lot farther in 1971 when he took over the entire front page with an editorial he wrote that he titled, "Will the Federal Bureaucracy Destroy Individual Freedom in America?" Over six columns he lambasted bureaucrats in Washington, DC. He wrote that there are three great parties—Democrat, Republican and Federal bureaucracy. "Of the three," he wrote, "the Federal bureaucracy is the strongest and most powerful because it is the best organized and is protected from political reprisal by civil service." He wrote that when a new administration takes over, less that 10 percent of the bureaucrats leave and 90 percent keep their jobs regardless of which party is in power. Quotations about freedom from famous persons in history covered page two, and the regular front page began on page three. He felt so strongly about the subject that he ran the editorial again in the Sesquicentennial edition of July 4, 1976.

Pulliam was an active Republican, but many of his friends were Democrats. He played golf regularly on Saturdays with Charles H. Boswell, the city's mayor (1959-62). He became a close friend of President Lyndon Johnson and Governor Branigin (1965-68). After JFK became president, he even grew to like him personally. But beyond party politics, Pulliam was a staunch conservative. He and other Chamber of Commerce types in those years saw the Federal government's growth as threatening. As a result, Indiana made little effort to obtain Federal funds, while other states feasted at the Federal trough. Even interstate highways were late coming to the state.

There were other groups that he distrusted. In his biography of his grandfather, Russ Pulliam wrote that "past experience with lawyers and bankers made him antagonistic to them. His will decreed that neither lawyers nor bankers could be involved in running his newspapers after his death. Lawyers, he observed, seemed quick to kill stories for fear of libel; bankers were too interested in profit."

Most of the memos that came from Phoenix, where Pulliam had settled, were sent to the managing editor, Bob Early. If the target happened to be a politician of either party whom he thought needed a spanking, Early often passed the order on to Lester Hunt, the paper's talented hatchet man. Many of the other directives went to the news editor or the city editor to carry out.

His editorial page editors, Jameson G. Campaigne at *The Star* and M. Stanton Evans at *The News*, carried out his conservative views on their pages.

When the Watergate scandal was dominating front pages in 1973, he sent a memo to managing editors of both papers. Dated July 31, 1973, it read, "Dear Boys: I don't agree with Lugar and Bowen entirely about the press overplaying Watergate but I do think the *Star* and *News* have done their share in letting Watergate overshadow the other news. So let's start playing it down some. There's other news being made each day." A year later Nixon resigned.

In a memo to Early dated Aug. 4, 1970, he wrote:

> I have just been talking to Gene and told him I was fed up by the *Star* Statehouse reporting on this endless picking on the Governor. I want this needling of Whitcomb (Edgar) stopped until after the election. It's just asinine the way this nit-picking on everything he does is written day after day.
>
> It's going to be hard enough to beat Hartke this Fall anyway and I want them to lay off until after the election. We sure as hell can't beat Hartke if we split or help to split the Republican Party.

I have to wonder if the state would be flooded with riverboat casinos if ECP had been alive when the Indiana General Assembly authorized them. In 1964 he sent a memo jointly to Early and Bob Collins, the sports editor. It stated,

> You will probably be getting some pressure from Joe Quinn in an effort to get our support for pari-mutuel betting and the

> answer is "NO". We haven't fought it—we're not going to make a big noise about it but if they introduce this bill in the legislature, we're certainly going to oppose it. So don't let him creep up on the soft side of you and get you halfway committed before you know what we're going to do for we are certainly going to be opposed to it. The main reason I'm opposed to it is that the embezzlement rate in Louisville where they have pari-mutual (sic) betting is about four times what it is here in Indianapolis. Betting makes petty thieves out of too many weak hearted people. It causes anguish all over the place.

In another directive to editors and managing editors of both papers he wrote:

> Also I think we have to keep riding this crusade for the conviction and punishment of those hoodlums and thugs around town. Practically nobody has been punished. I think that sooner or later we've got to put this up to Mayor Lugar to come back home from cloud 59 where he has been floating around and keep his promise to restore law and order to Indianapolis. He's done a good job on all fronts but hasn't done a damn thing on that. The muggings, robbings and rapings are worse now than they were six months ago. The main thing is to keep everlasting at it. Let's have either a news story or an editorial at least 2 or 3 times a week until the legislature convenes. Also, follow up every arrest and see why the people aren't brought to trial. If we could get about 25 or 30 of these hoodlums sent to jail with heavy sentences, the muggings and robberies in this town would be reduced 50 percent.

Pulliam may have been the crusading publisher, but he was a businessman first. In 65 years in journalism, he bought and sold 51 papers, most of them struggling dailies and weeklies that he would improve and sell. The first major daily he bought was *The Star* in 1944. He bought it for $2.35 million.

He acquired the *Muncie Star* and the *Muncie Press* that year, as well, and two years later he purchased the *Arizona Republic* and *Phoenix Gazette* for $4 million—"the best buy I ever made." Phoenix was just beginning its phenomenal growth when he bought the papers. He liked to say "it was like marrying a Rockefeller." When he acquired *The Indianapolis News* in 1948 it was the 51st and last paper he purchased.

By then he had come a long way in his journalistic quests. He was born in a dugout (a mud hut) in Ulysses, Kansas. His father, Reverend Irvin Brown Pulliam, was a Methodist frontier missionary. By age 15 Pulliam had lived in 10 small towns.

He enrolled at DePauw University, the alma mater of his mother, Martha Collins Pulliam, but he left after his junior year. Before leaving, though, he and nine other students founded Sigma Delta Chi, the nation's oldest journalism fraternity. Now known as the Society of Professional Journalists, it was formed to establish standards to make journalism respectable. He also started the *DePauw Daily* campus newspaper.

He became editor of the *Atchison (*Kansas) *Champion* in 1911 and a year later his father helped him buy controlling interest in the paper. At 23 he owned his first daily.

By then he was married to his college sweetheart, Myrta Smith of Noblesville. She died in 1917 of complications from a miscarriage. He later married Martha Ott of Franklin. After he bought the *Lebanon Reporter*, they settled in Lebanon for 15 years. In 1941 he divorced her and married his secretary, Nina Mason, who had been associated with Pulliam papers since being named secretary-treasurer and a director of Central Newspapers Inc. in 1929

Russell Pulliam got no cooperation from Nina when he wrote the biography of his grandfather. She died in 1997 at age 91. She willed all of her Central Newspaper stock to the Nina Mason Pulliam Charitable Trust, which she established to make grants to charitable institutions. The trust was valued at more than $400 million at the beginning of 2000.

¤

3 • Terror In The Newsroom

When Gene Pulliam bought *The Star* in 1944 one of his first moves was to name Robert P. Early as managing editor. Early had been a desk pounding city editor for a couple of years, and he became a desk pounding managing editor. He continued pounding in that position for 34 years, terrorizing the staff — and some other department heads — often with obscenity-laced outbursts.

He had been with the paper since 1927 and he conducted his job as managing editor much like it was done in the 1920s—loud and demanding. In Early's case, it was certainly true that news is whatever the managing editor says it is. And just about anything else, as well.

But in fairness, it was Early who turned an undistinguished newspaper into a prize-winning daily. He did it with undermanned staffs, and with a publisher who had his own set of goals and demands.

Early was a handsome Irish Catholic with a full head of hair. As managing editor he always wore a suit and tie while the other male staffers worked in shirtsleeves. He had two extraordinary assets—his energy and his memory. Make a mistake and it maybe brought up a decade later. But he was loyal to his staff and backed it if he thought one of the reporters had been unfairly criticized or mistreated.

Bob Early chats with Irving Leibowitz, managing editor of the Indianapols Times, *and Leibo's wife "Plum."*

He demanded that the reporters get the facts, get them first, and tell them in clear unadorned prose. He had little regard for creativity. *The Star* went for hard news. We left any analyzing of the news to the editorial page crew.

Early was a micro-manager who ruled the staff by fear. He made the major—and sometimes minor—decisions and the staff carried out his orders. In the newsroom it was always, "What does Early want?"

He bellowed if the *Indianapolis Times* or *The News* broke a story first. The business editor, Ralph N. Moore, before my time, was the glad-handing Chamber type. I was told that Early saw the lead story on page one in *The News* about Eli Lilly & Co. buying the Curtis-Wright plant after the war. "What about this, Ralph?" Early asked. "Oh, I've known about this for two weeks." It was the wrong answer.

He wanted every score and every local story in the paper, even if it meant the paper would be late coming off the presses. Blame the printers, never the editorial department. Holding a news story for a day or two was unacceptable.

Our stylebook reflected many of Early's taboos. No photos of rats or snakes allowed. The word stink was a no-no. Despite his own obscene-laced outbursts, he prohibited cursing or profanity or even damn and hell in the paper. Early was something of a sexual puritan, so no sexual innuendo was permitted. It was gasoline, not gas, and it was a grocery store, not a grocery. We were reminded regularly that it was State Avenue, not State Street, that Broadway stood alone, and the difference between flout and flaunt. And it was never INDY in a headline. No nicknames and it was always full name and middle initial or the copy went back to the reporter.

Reporters were to get bylines on their stories only if they were outstanding—and certainly never more than one per issue; both directives generally ignored as he grew older.

There were few fields that Early didn't feel competent to enter. He could be a detective, a psychologist, constitutional law expert, an economist, a criminologist, medical expert, park planner, and guardian of the public's right to know–and, of course, *The Star's* right, too. You didn't discuss or converse with Bob Early. You listened. If he had a sense of humor, he rarely brought it to the office.

Golf was the one hobby he enjoyed and he was always ready with advice. The sports editor, Bob Collins, said he was in Early's office one afternoon and was being given advice on the proper golf grip when the telephone rang. It was someone from the production department complaining about the sports copy holding up the city edition press run. Early disagreed, telling the caller that the problem was due to lazy printers. After roaring at the caller for five minutes, he slammed the receiver at the cradle. It missed and he slammed it again, then calmly walked from behind the desk and said to Bob, "Now, if you just move your hands into this position..."

I was told that when he was city editor, the glass tops on the desks were replaced with plastic because he broke too many of them.

Early was a fixture at *The Star* for 54 years. He graduated from Cathedral High School in 1923. He began his journalism career as a summertime office boy at the paper in the World War I years. He went to work in 1925 for the United Press news service in Indianapolis. He then spent a year working on the *Connersville News-Examiner* before joining *The Star* in 1927. He worked many of the reporting beats for 13 years before being named an assistant city editor in 1941 and promoted to city editor in 1944, a job he held until Pulliam named him managing editor two years later.

His older brother, Maurice Early, who joined *The Star* in 1916, wrote a page-one political column, "The Day in Indiana" from 1939 until shortly before he died in 1954. Another brother, the Reverend Francis J. Early, was pastor of Holy Spirit Catholic Church on the city's eastside. Father Early was known to have an explosive temper, too, though his language was not as obscenity laced as his brother's.

Early read the paper thoroughly. There was no item too small to get his attention, though I sometimes thought he might have picked out errors on minor stories to give the impression that nothing escaped him.

He had a hotline telephone to the city desk. Those of us working on the desk dreaded hearing it ring. It usually meant more work for desk editors, forcing them to drop whatever they were doing to carry out an order. Very often he was raising hell about a story, demanding that it be expanded or shortened or rewritten.

When Al McCord, an assistant city editor, would be on the receiving end of one of Early's tirades that might wind up, "goddamnit send someone out there to straighten out that c........" Al would softly respond to each of the orders and after Early had hung up, Al would slam the receiver into the cradle, often missing a couple of times.

"A certain amount of controlled turmoil is necessary to any operation," Early remarked. "It keeps people alert, rather than letting them slack off and think they can do less than their best."

But it wasn't always controlled turmoil on his part. Once when he went to the paper's library to get the text from the Bible for an Easter prayer for the front page, he discovered the page had been torn from it. He came storming into the city room bellowing,"Who the goddamned hell has been fucking with the goddamned Bible."

Early was very protective of his role as managing editor. One busy Saturday afternoon in the newsroom he called me several times from his home with instructions on which reporter he wanted to report on a story about the switch that night to daylight savings time. We were shorthanded and the reporter was buried working two other stories, so I assigned it to another reporter. That angered him and after about four calls, I finally told him, "Get off my back." It was the closest I ever stood up to him.

He said, "Wait right there." Then he got in his car, drove 10 miles to the paper, called me into his office and lectured me (the city editor) about the need to follow orders, specifically his orders. I couldn't believe it. A psychologist probably had an answer. I'm sure that night was one of those when I woke up angry at 3 o'clock telling myself that if the SOB died I wouldn't even attend his funeral. But as the years have softened my views, I'd have to admit Bob Early helped to make me a decent newspaperman and that he was behind most of my promotions.

He was not always so sure of himself as he liked us all to believe. Bill Dyer, the general manager, said he received a late night call from him a few months after he became managing editor. "Bill, this is Early," Dyer said he recalled. "The guy from the *Register and Tribune* syndicate was in. He wanted to sell the Oursler series [a Lenten story by novelist Fulton Oursler that the syndicate had reworked as an Advent feature] and get the guy bumped off at Christmas. I told him to stick it up his ass."

It wasn't only the staff that felt his ire.

A new Lamson tube system was installed in the building to permit copy to be sent and received rapidly in the various departments. It was much like the tube system used at drive-in banks today. It replaced an old metal basket that carried copy to the composing room on an electrical pulley system. The Lamson system developed problems. On one occasion it could be traced to some clown sending a soft drink can through the system and it got stuck. But there were other problems with the system so Golden Faris, the paper's production superintendent, brought in a troubleshooter from the Lamson company to work out the glitches. The two of them went to Early's office to discuss the problems. The Lamson man opened the session by telling Early that it was necessary for him to gain some control and discipline over the staff. With that Early came out of his chair and lectured the guy for 30 minutes.

When he left the office, the troubleshooter said to Farris,"I guess I said the wrong thing, eh?"

While he reigned, *The Star* annually received most of the major journalism awards in the state, as well as some national awards.

For its coverage of the disaster at the Fairgrounds Coliseum in 1963 the paper received the coveted National Headliner Award. Early left his office to direct the coverage from the newsroom. It happened on Halloween night. A propane tank exploded sending concrete stands 50 feet in the air during the finale of a Holiday on Ice show. It took the lives of 74 spectators and wounded more than 400 others. That tragedy will be covered later in this book.

That same year he and political reporter Lester Hunt directed a campaign that benefited all forms of media in the state when the Indiana General Assembly enacted the Anti-Secrecy Act, forcing the state to open its records to the public.

Under his direction, reporters in 1957 exposed payoffs in the State Highway Department in connection with highway contracts during the administration of Governor George N. Craig. Initially, reporters failed to uncover the scandal but Early insisted they continued to probe. It eventually paid off in stories of a major scandal.

The paper's exposéof corruption in the Indianapolis Police Department in 1974 was backed by Early. After six months of investigation, a team of reporters and photographers produced several hundred stories over the next few months. The work brought the paper its first Pulitzer Prize, along with 17 others awards, including six national honors.

When Early wasn't issuing orders to the staff, he was receiving orders from the publisher, generally for the paper to go after some politician, almost always a Democrat.

Twice in October 1970 when I was city editor I received detailed memos from ECP via Early on ways to defeat Senator Vance Hartke and Congressman Andy Jacobs Jr., both Democrats, of course. One of the orders read, "Get a shot of Senator Hartke with Coretta King. Arrange for a reporter to be along to ask Hartke, 'Just how do you stand on busing, Senator Hartke?' Make certain that the question is asked in the presence of Mrs. King."

We had three reporters trying to carry out the Hartke-Jacobs directives. One of them, Jep Cadou Jr., labeled them "Overkill Memos 101 A and B."

The editorial cartoons by a prize-winning cartoonist Charley Werner almost always reflected Pulliam's conservative political views. The only time I ever heard Werner being in disfavor with Pulliam was the time he drew a cartoon after the Russians sent the first satellite (Sputnik) into space in 1957. The cartoon showed President Eisenhower hunting for his golf ball in the rough with caption above saying simply, "Sputnik." Early usually selected the Werner cartoon as the dominant page one art unless an outstanding photo was available. *The Star* was one of the last papers still running editorial cartoons on the front page, a longtime practice of the ultra-conservative *Chicago Tribune* in those years.

Politicians, especially if they were Democrats, were frequent targets. They were usually vulnerable and reluctant to retaliate. Early had no compunction about ordering a reporter or editor to get a comment from the mayor, the governor or the sheriff or the police chief about some story that was developing. It made no difference whether it was midnight or later, we'd rout them out of bed. But no late night calls to influential citizens or to advertisers.

Each year that the Indiana General Assembly met we would assign six persons to cover the proceedings in the Statehouse. The staff dutifully reported on the status of the major bills, as well as listing each of the bills introduced and as they progressed through the system. It was a tedious job but because *The Star* was the largest paper in the state and the legislature met in Indianapolis it fell to the paper to accept that responsibility. I questioned whether the subscribers bothered to read the stories and roundups and lists but we liked to think we were the paper of record.

If our reporting turned up some problem in the state, we could count on Early's ordering a reporter to induce a legislator to sponsor a bill to rectify the problem. While I may have been part of the process, I sometimes wondered if all of those bills designed to correct a specific problem were a waste of time, money and effort; that we'd have been better off letting some local agency handle it. Pushing a bill or bills through the legislature was a way to keep the story alive and to demonstrate the paper's clout.

During one session we pushed for a highway measure that Early felt was vital. We'd get a call two or three times a week asking about the status of Bill 1145 or whatever. A reporter would have to run down the sponsor to get a line on it and report back. There was little interest in the legislature to pass the measure but on the final day of the session we were able to report to Early that the bill was enacted. That satisfied him, though I don't think he ever learned, as the bureau did later, that we had the wrong number on the bill.

Early was more permissive with the sports department. It was OK for athletes to regularly "ink a pact" in a sports headline, but the mayor never "inked" a pact. The sports staff operated in an office away from the newsroom, giving the staff a certain amount of privacy; enough certainly to hide the occasional drinking. One night when Early spotted some empty whiskey bottles in a drawer in the department, he asked Cy McBride, the assistant sports editor, "What are you doing with these things?" Cy quickly countered, "We're going to use them as candle holders." "Well, get rid of them," Early said and walked out.

Early usually came to his office around 3 o'clock in the afternoon. He oversaw the page one conference in his office about 5 o'clock. He left about 6 o'clock to have dinner at home, and he was back by 9:30 when the first edition (bulldog) arrived. He might leave at midnight or be in the office until 3 a.m.

In addition to the syndicate salesmen who learned to call on him late at night to tout a new comic strip or a bridge column, sycophants dropped by to massage his ego. They were politicians, lawyers, public relations practitioners, and a few old friends from his years as a reporter or from the neighborhood of his childhood. Most had axes to grind. One cloying publicist managed to get in the pictures of whatever group he was promoting and he had the sole distinction of being the only PR man in the city with an unlisted telephone number. His wife was a member of the humane society board of directors and she felt the animals weren't getting enough sympathetic treatment at the animal shelter. Fellow board members generally ignored her. But her husband believed he could make points with Early if he could get an expose of the shelter in *The Star*. So we were ordered to assign a cub reporter to apply for a job at the shelter so that he could get an inside look at conditions there.

It fell to Nick Peters to get the job. Nick was a young, handsome Ivy League type who had done his cub reporting on the police beat and was ready for more important journalism. The poor guy got the assignment, spending two weeks shoveling euthanized animals into the incinerator. It brought a few ineffectual demands from animal lovers to stop the practice. It was enough journalism for Nick. He soon moved on.

One particularly odious visitor was a resident of the suburban town of Lawrence. He was dirty and generally unkempt with a wispy mustache. He always carried a briefcase full of documents concerning water rates in Lawrence. It was his crusade that the utility needed a thorough investigation, and it fell to *The Star* to periodically report on whatever new disclosures he could produce. He began to feel so important that he began calling reporters and giving them orders on what leads they should pursue. A total waste of time.

Early had a soft spot for former reporters who had fallen on hard times, most of them victims of alcohol abuse. They would return to the city and visit Early for one last chance. We took them on and they usually lasted a week or two until their first paycheck arrived.

When I began at the paper Ross Nelson was the telegraph editor. He was one of the cadre that held the paper together during the war. Ross had a drinking problem, but he survived because Early wasn't much for firing people, especially any of the crew who were with him during the war.

One afternoon when he was returning from another liquid lunch, Ross was struck by a car just outside the building while crossing New York Street at the corner of Pennsylvania Street. Early decided that Ross was a victim of the walk-wait signs being placed too high on the light standards; so high in fact that Ross and other people could not read them. So we had to embark on a brief campaign to get the sign lowered. When we learned what it would cost to lower the signs throughout the city, the campaign ended at New York Street.

At the Press Club's annual Gridiron Dinner, which I chaired in 1979, one of the girls circulating throughout the dinner carrying placards with political barbs was carrying one that read: "Connor Wants Early Retirement." I had no knowledge of the sign and was never informed that I would be in line for his job. The sign embarrassed me but I had to chuckle when I saw it. My wife, Patty, was seated at the table with Bob and Helen Early. She, too, got a discreet laugh out of the sign but she said there was no reaction from the Earlys.

But it may have had some effect. He retired later that year. He was 74 years old, still strong and given no indication that he planned to step down. The Earlys moved to Phoenix in 1981 where their son and daughter lived. He died in 1986 of a lung ailment. He was 81.

I did attend the memorial service for him in Indianapolis.

¤

4 • Oh, Those Campaigns

Bob Early came up with a number of campaigns over the years to improve Indianapolis.

When I started at the paper in 1949 Yard Parks (the "make your yard a park") campaign was flourishing. The campaign was Early's reaction to a claim by author John Gunther in his best-selling book *Inside USA* that Indianapolis was the "dirtiest city in the U.S."

He can't get away with that, Early decided, so he enlisted the help of Mrs. B. Lynn Adams, a woman of strong will and presence in the community, to direct the Yard Parks campaign. The campaign seemed to run on endlessly. Over time B. Lynn twisted enough arms to produce 32 divisions in the crusade. Among those whose arms were twisted were the city's park department, restaurants, drive-ins, industrial firms, small businesses, truckers — just about any group that pledged to do its part to beautify the city. Her disciples began by clearing yards and vacant lots and gutters of paper cups, beer and soft drink bottles, and then they went to work planting trees and flowers. It was a sensible and effective campaign. Those signing on could count on getting the names of their firms in the paper, and Mrs. Adams made sure they carried out their pledge to do their part in helping to clean up the city.

B. Lynn conducted contests for the cleanest efforts at drive-ins, and factories and service stations. She enlisted thousands of boys and girls to participate in spring cleanup efforts.

Each of these deeds had to be recorded in the pages of *The Star* and it was a job of the staff to come up with a new take on the program each time Early asked, "What have we got on Yard Parks?"

If the answer was a reluctant "nothing," Early managed to come up with an angle that some hapless reporter was told to develop into a story to keep the campaign rolling.

Early believed that we had to hammer the reader day after day to get results. He may have been right, though I always felt that readers ignored the stories—unless, of course, they were mentioned in them. And it was dreary work for the reporters assigned to the campaigns.

But the payoffs came when Indianapolis received the Clean City award from the National Clean-up, Paint-up, Fix-up Bureau.

So there, Mr.Gunther.

After Yard Parks did its job of helping to beautify the city, Early was ready to save the lives of its motorists. He embarked on the "Daylight Running Lights" campaign. He got the idea in 1963 from an item in Lowell Nussbaum's daily human interest column, "The Things I Hear." A suggestion from a reader of his column that cars, particularly light-colored cars, would be easier for oncoming drivers to see during the daytime if there was a light centered on their grills. Early thought it was an idea worth pursuing.

So we embarked on a campaign to sell motorists on the value of installing the inexpensive lights. Soon the lights were manufactured and they began showing up on thousands of cars, some of them in other states. Despite studies proving that the lights were scientifically sound, we could not convince Detroit to install them on new cars.

Not that we didn't try. I later counted 92 stories that we had run about the safety device. Day after day we dragooned someone to keep the campaign alive by indorsing the idea or proving its worth scientifically. Traffic safety officials were brought into the net, and so were optometrists, politicians, service clubs and truckers. Even Rodger Ward, two-time winner of the 500-Mile Race, was induced to indorse the campaign.

Throughout 1963 the question at the page one conference was, "What have we got on running lights?"

I don't know if the campaign could claim any responsibility for it, but years later cars coming off the assembly lines were equipped with low-level headlights that stayed on during daylight hours.

The campaign enabled me to pick up a few dollars when the *National Observer*, a national weekly newspaper for which I was Indiana stringer, called one day to ask that I get the paper a story about them. Barney Kilgore, publisher of the *Wall Street Journal* and the *Observer*, said he'd seen some of the little lights on cars and wondered what it was all about.

Of all of Early's campaigns, I'd rank the Ruins at Holliday Park as the most troublesome. It was a project that attracted his attention off and on for 20 years.

Indianapolis's celebrated artist, Elmer E. Taflinger, designed the Ruins. "Taf" managed to get commissioned to design a setting for three limestone statues, which had adorned the St. Paul building in New York City that was erected in 1898. The five-foot statues of three kneeling men depicting the three Races of Mankind were up for bidding when Western Electric decided to raze the building in 1958 to make way for a new headquarters.

The United Nations, a New York airport and universities bid for the statues but Indianapolis got them, influenced perhaps by the fact that Karl T. Bitter, an Indianapolis native, had sculpted them.

The statues were to be erected in one of the city's parks but with changes in the city administrations and other delays work was held off until the 1970s. Taflinger, another of Early's late evening visitors, sought press coverage for his extravagant plans, so the city desk got repeated orders from Early to have someone talk to Taf about the latest wrinkle in his plans.

And there were plenty of wrinkles, particularly his effort to get assistance from the park department. When Taf complained to Early that he was having difficulty getting cooperation from the department, we'd get an order from Early to have a reporter "get to the bottom of this."

Taflinger named his design Constitution Mall. It included three limestone tablets representing the three races of mankind and three branches of government, a reflecting pool with fountains, 25 Grecian columns salvaged from a former convent, and four statues of allegorical females from the old Marion County Courthouse—all to be situated in a tree-filled landscapes with Bitter's statues hovering over the pool atop a backdrop.

Taflinger's intention was to make the entire setting seem weathered and ancient in a ruins setting.

It became the job of the city desk to assign some unlucky reporter to track the project step by step. A cub reporter generally got the assignment. In time, Taflinger became bold enough to order the reporter to write about any changes in his design and to pressure the park department to move ahead with the work.

The Ruins were finally completed in 1979. It became the duty of the city desk to encourage visitors with lavish stories. But I thought Taflinger had gone too far when he complained to Early one evening that children had been throwing Frisbees in the park, annoying visitors viewing The Ruins. I got a call from Early telling me to have a reporter talk to Taflinger and work up a story saying the parks department should prohibit the kids from playing near The Ruins. That was one order I ignored.

Taf's Ruins have fallen into disrepair over the years but they're still standing—and the kids are still tossing Frisbees in the park.

¤

5 • An In-House Detective

Bob Early liked to solve lingering murder cases from his office. If the cops weren't having any success, Early would dream up a possible scenario and send reporters out to confirm his clues (or "clews" as he would have us spell it). He was often urged on by his sidekick, Charley Griffo. "Griff" held a series of editing positions over the years but his first love was solving crimes.

To keep a story alive, Early would come up with a theory and then have the police reporter induce some patsy in the police department or mayor's office to say that the department was investigating.

In a light-hearted memoir he wrote a few years ago, Jim Mitchell told of being assigned to cover a murder in Brownsburg, a murder that was baffling the three-man Brownsburg police department. The year was 1954.

Jim said Early stepped in and the story jumped from back in the paper to the split page and eventually to page one. "Why?" Jim writes, "Because Managing Editor Early had figured out WHODONIT. Without ever leaving his downtown office."

Early assigned Jim to do the reporting on the story. Jim wrote:

"All we had to do was write our stuff with such skill that even those dodoes at the Brownsburg police station would catch on that the local dentist had committed the crime."

Mitchell said Early instructed him to take careful notes as he "conducted our nightly discussion" of the day's new developments.

Jim wrote, "We ran two days along these lines, getting bolder each day with our innuendoes regarding the good dentist. Early became firmer in his conviction [that the doctor did it]. Mitchell's knees grew weaker and weaker by the minute. This was fantasy journalism. Every day. On Page One. He knew it was wrong. He knew he wanted out. He did not know how to make his escape.

"The solution to his problem was not long in presenting itself. On the third day of this madness...10 minutes after the daily conference in Early's office Mitchell's telephone rang.

> "Is this Mitchell? Listen very carefully. I will say what I have to say just once. I won't call again. I have a gun and if you ignore me tonight I will come visit you tomorrow. I know that you live at 5825 Hillside Avenue. I know that you have a wife and four children. I drove along Hillside past your home this afternoon. I know right where it is."

> "Wait a minute. Who is this? Why are you threatening me?"
>
> "I will introduce myself. I am Dr.—. I'm the Brownsburg dentist who, for some unknown reason, you are trying to convict as a murderer. I know you have been writing the libelous trash about me in the paper. Now I want those stories to stop. I am not a murderer. But I have a gun and I intend to bring it with me when I pay my visit up on Hillside Avenue…if you don't stop calling me a murderer in print. Now. Tonight. Goodby."

Mitchell said he walked into Early's office, dropped his entire file on the case and refused the assignment for the first time in his life. He thought he might be resigning his job, too. But Early came to his senses, Mitchell said, and the story was dropped.

Jim said he never felt the same again about city desk employment at *The Star*, so when a public relations position "beckoned from Butler University, he leaped. Never again returning to newspapering."

¤

6 • A Stagnant City

The city that *The Star* was covering in the 1950s wasn't much to brag about. It would be 30 years before Indianapolis could begin to erase the label that critics gave it — Indy-No-Place. But Indianapolis was not alone in its stagnancy. Most of the country was just beginning to recover from two momentous events of the century—a devastating Depression and World War II. For 30 years the country had been on hold.

Downtown Indianapolis looked much like it had when the banks failed in 1929. There hadn't been a new building erected in downtown Indianapolis since the Circle Tower on Monument Circle went up in 1930. And years of heating with coal had left a veneer of soot on the buildings. The streets earned one of the mayors, Charles H. Boswell, the designation, "Chuckhole Charley." Trash lined the gutters.

John Gunther angered its citizens when he rated Indianapolis as "the dirtiest city in the U.S." in his best-selling book, *Inside USA*. He may have been right.

Downtown Indianapolis seemed to shut down when the sun went down. It wasn't muggers that kept its streets deserted. Downtown simply had few attractions. Nine movie theaters and a few undistinguished restaurants were about all it could offer after dark, and even most of the movie houses wouldn't be around much longer. And blaming it on television came later. There were a few drive-in restaurants on the edges of the city, but the McDonalds and their copiers came later. Eating out was pretty much confined to birthdays and anniversaries. The state's liquor laws didn't help. Visitors soured on the city when they couldn't buy a drink after midnight and none at all on Sunday. With those restrictions, there was little incentive for opening nightclubs. Most socializing was done in private clubs.

We were driving Chevys, Fords and Plymouths, giving turn signals with left arms out of the window. It would have been unthinkable that we'd be driving Japanese-made cars in a few years. They were still "dirty Japs." We drove with the windows open because cars lacked air conditioning. And so did our homes. Men wore double-breasted suits and fedoras, and women wore skirts and dresses that ended below their knees.

There was a shortage of houses and apartments. Indiana University Extension classes were being held in a building at Michigan and Delaware streets. The Knights of Pythias building would soon be leveled to make room for the Indiana National Bank tower, the city's tallest. The Indianapolis Press Club was prospering in its second-floor quarters above the Canary Cottage on Monument Circle.

Elvis was on his way with "Heartbreak Hotel" and Patti Page was singing about "That Doggie in the Window." Marlon Brando was moaning "I coulda been somebody" in *On The Waterfront,* and *The Catcher In The Rye* was on every college student's reading list. Dads spent their nights out in bowling alleys. And you'd have to visit a carnival to find men with tattoos and ponytails.

It was a time before sex sold every product ... before the ambulance chasers made their pitches on TV... and before we were advised to "ask your doctor."

Television had its critics as early as 1950. Boston University President Daniel Marsh declared that, "If the television craze continues with the present level of programs, we are destined to have a nation of morons."

In his book, Gunther had this to say about the city:

"Indianapolis is an unkempt city, unswept, raw, a terrific place for basketball and auto racing, a former pivot of the Ku-Kluxers, and in it you may see the second ugliest monument in the world."

Gunther didn't name either of the two monuments but we surmised the second place went to the Soldiers and Sailors monument on The Circle. Few of us saw it that way. It was the place to meet downtown. It was the city's security blanket.

I can't remember thinking Indianapolis was all that bad. People tend to feel that where they live is the center of the universe. With friends and family here and my new job at the paper, I liked the place.

The war had a big impact on the city's economy. War plants had been busy and the trend of local businesses being bought up or merged to become divisions of larger companies had not yet begun.

The city had only four banks and their owners liked it that way. They had the support of the Indiana General Assembly in enacting laws prohibiting cross-county banking. The bankers felt secure until they realized the rest of the country was not adhering to such restrictions and banks were being bought and merged, putting the squeeze on smaller banks.

The bankers were not the only community bosses who liked their little monopolies and fought a rear-guard action against outsiders, and that included the Federal government. Spokesman for that moneyed clique was William Henry Book, a little man with a big brain. He held the title of executive vice president of the Indianapolis Chamber of Commerce. His job ostensibly was to serve the Chamber's members but, in truth, they served him and did his bidding. Whenever there was a threat to the city's normalcy by some non-Chamber entrepreneur with plans for disturbing the status quo, we'd get the word from Bob Early to "see what Bill Book thinks about this." Book's usual response was either "Do we really need this?" or "Let's hold the line on this one."

Book became director of government research for the chamber in 1926 after a brief reporting stint with *The Indianapolis News.* During the administration of Governor Paul V. McNutt in the 1930s he served as administrator of relief. He became convinced that Roosevelt's New Deal was heading the country toward socialism, and so began his career of opposing an intrusive Federal government.

When Book returned to the Chamber he became a home rule advocate. It was just what the wealthy old families running the city liked to hear. The city and state's conservatives fought the social and economic reforms of the New Deal throughout the 1940s and 1950s. Book represented what was wrong with the city. The city needed visionaries and it wasn't getting them from the Chamber of Commerce at that time. There was no talk of big dreams for Indianapolis. "What's wrong with the way things are!" and "Who needs Washington!" were the accepted answers. It was a wait-and-see time. The fears the Depression brought were still with us.

The Chamber could count on the support of Eugene C. Pulliam and his newspapers. The editorial pages of *The St*ar, and even page one on occasion, reflected Pulliam's conservatism. In its provincial view, Indianapolis didn't need the Federal government's help, even if the rest of the country was reaching for its share of Washington's dollars.

The paper supported its U. S. senators, both rigid Republican conservatives. Shaming the state was Senator William E. Jenner. Considered a disgrace by virtually every liberal and most Democrats, Jenner had his admirers in the Republican Party. He was a strong supporter of Senator Joseph McCarthy, who was elected to the Senate in 1946, the same year that he was elected. An alcoholic, McCarthy was ruthlessly exploiting the nation's fear of communism by smearing the State Department as a haven for Reds. McCarthy found it effective to wave his purported list of "card-carrying communists" until the Senate finally shut him up.

Jenner had a foul mouth and many of his political attacks were vitriolic, but he angered even fellow Republicans in 1950 when he charged General George C. Marshall with being a "front for traitors" and "a living lie" after he "lost" China to the Reds. This was the man who was the nation's highest ranking general during the war, a former secretary of state, and father of the Marshall Plan that helped to rebuild Europe after the war.

Not vitriolic like Jenner, the state's other senator, Homer E. Capehart, rarely deviated from his conservatism during the 18 years he served in the Senate. I don't remember much of what distinguished Capehart but I do remember the day that we ran a picture of him with a pig at the State Fair and the art lines saying "Capehart (right)". I never learned whether it was deliberate or just sloppy editing.

The city's image was further tarnished when a former candy manufacturer, Robert Welch, organized the fanatic right-wing John Birch Society here on Dec. 9, 1958. Welch added to the Cold War rhetoric by calling President Eisenhower a "card-carrying communist."

The state and city were provincial and puritanical. Cotton Mather would have felt at home here. The closets that gays inhabited were not only closed, they were locked. Single mothers had their own closets. "The Establishment" frowned on long hair, beards, Afros, rock 'n roll and, of course, the gyrations of Elvis. There was a fear or distrust of outsiders and *The Star's* editorial pages reflected that distrust. "The good old days" were best.

Indianapolis liked to think of itself as a good place to raise a family, but it wasn't such a good place for its black citizens who were living in restrictive ghetto areas. And blacks were about 20 percent of the population. There were shameful slums west of the downtown area where people lived without indoor plumbing in shacks that didn't come down until Indiana and Purdue universities relocated their regional campuses there under the cumbersome title of Indiana University-Purdue University at Indianapolis (IUPUI) in the 1970s. The Indianapolis Water Company's canal ran through the area on its way to White River. Until the university arrived, the canal attracted old tires, baby buggies, sofas and often bodies. Thirty years later the same canal—sanitized—had become the major feature in the new White River State Park in downtown Indianapolis.

There was a shortage of decent housing in the 1950s, making it difficult for returning veterans with young wives to find a place to live. While covering City Hall in 1952 I wrote about a jackleg minister renting three garages to couples in an alley a mile from Monument Circle. He charged each couple $65 a month. The garages did have paved floors. The shortage of housing and the condition of many of them was being addressed by a new agency in City Hall named the Redevelopment Commission.

Public transportation was surrendering to the automobile. In 1949 you could ride a streetcar, a bus or a trackless trolley for 11 cents and 2 cents if you wanted to transfer to another line. But on January 10, 1953, the last streetcar ran and four years later the trackless trolleys were gone, too.

In contrast, Indianapolis at the turn of the 20th century had its share of elegant restaurants, fine bars, theaters and hotels, and scores of private clubs. The city was known as a literary center. Novelists Booth Tarkington and Meredith Nicholson and poet James Whitcomb Riley were among the nation's heralded literary figures. But two world wars and a depression had radically changed the place.

George E. Kessler, the nation's premier park planner and landscape designer, was hired in 1908 to devise a parkway plan along Fall Creek and White River. Kessler, though, had a grander plan, one that called for parkways along Pleasant Run and Pogue's Run, as well. His idea was to give the citizens a convenient and attractive way to reach the city's 12 municipal parks. He added the sunken gardens at Garfield Park and built bridges in Brookside Park. He designed one of the city's more attractive roadways on the northside. When completed in 1929 it was named Kessler Boulevard in his honor.

But there was little to brag about the city's cultural attractions by mid-century. The city's meager art collections were housed in the Herron Museum of Art at 16th and Pennsylvania streets. Indianapolis had only two legitimate theaters, the Civic and the Murat, but its symphony orchestra was well regarded.

St. Vincent Hospital was still treating patients at its building overlooking Fall Creek at Illinois Street, and Methodist Hospital's expansion had not begun. Blacks and gunshot victims went to General Hospital.

The city got its first shopping mall in 1957 when Eastgate opened on the city's eastern edge, and Glendale Mall followed on the northside a year later. The exodus to the suburbs was underway, and schools soon followed. North Central High School, the first of the major suburban schools, opened in 1956.

Indianapolis had every reason to brag about Crispus Attucks High School winning the state basketball tourney in 1955, 1956 and again in 1959. The school was the only Indianapolis school to have won the tourney, but the bragging was muted because Attucks was an all-black school.

Three of the mayors in the fifties, Alex M. Clark, Phillip L. Bayt and Charles H. Boswell, were personable, but they demonstrated little leadership. Clark, a Republican, was a genial lawyer and municipal court judge who became mayor without much interest in running the city. Democrats Bayt and Boswell played musical chairs with the office, both resigning (Bayt twice) to seek higher or more permanent jobs—all part of an intricate plan for control of the Democratic Party in Marion County. Boswell gave up control of the county committee to take the federal job of postmaster.

Both Bayt and Boswell were eager to please *The Star* and its publisher. Boswell, an outstanding golfer, regularly played golf with Pulliam on Saturday mornings. Bayt, fearful of what criticism—or praise—the paper might have for him or his administration, often showed up at the paper at 9:30 at night to get a copy of the bulldog edition. In truth, there never was much to say—good or bad—about Phil or his administration. (Phil did hold one enviable record—the only athlete at George Washington High School to letter in five different sports.)

In the mid-1960s John J. Barton, a former superintendent of state police, served as another pleasant mayor. Barton, too, was a Democrat. His administration's chief achievement was forming the Greater Indianapolis Progress Committee, a group of civic leaders who were charged with coming up with ways for the city to get off dead center. Barton's other achievement was bucking *The Star* and its conservative followers by going after some of the dollars leaving Washington. He used those dollars to build public housing projects for low-income families.

Efforts to clean up the city were helped in the 1960s when the major state and Federal buildings got rid of decades of coal soot by sandblasting.

The city didn't get effective leadership until Richard G. Lugar became mayor in 1968. A 35-year-old Rhodes scholar, Lugar was brilliant and articulate, and he enlisted several of the top young people from business and industry to work with him. His major accomplishment was getting a bill passed in the Indiana Legislature that consolidated the city and county governments. As a result of Uni-Gov, the city became the 12th largest city in the country, moving up from 26th place. It went from 82 square miles with 520,000 residents to 388 square miles and 792,000 residents.

After two terms, Lugar was elected to the U. S. Senate where he is serving his fourth term. A Presbyterian minister, William H. Hudnut III, succeeded him, serving four colorful and successful terms from 1976 to 1991. It was during his administrations that the city embarked on a bold strategy for the city to become the amateur sports capital of the U.S.

The city hosted the National Sports Festival in 1982, showing that it could carry off a major event. When Indianapolis landed the 1988 Pan Am Games, the rest of the country took notice. To stage the games, the city and state built a world-class natatorium and a top-rated track and field complex on the IUPUI campus, and the Major Taylor Velodrome for bicycle racing near the Marian College campus on the northwestside. The games ran for 16 days and each day we published stand-alone sections on them. We even brought in two Spanish-speaking reporters from the Arizona Republic to produce a daily wrap-up of events in Spanish.

Indianapolis did indeed become the amateur sports capital. The governing bodies of half a dozen sports moved their headquarters here, and in 1999 the National Collegiate Athletic Association followed suit.

Over the years the city brought in professional sports, and opened a convention center. The day of disdaining Federal dollars was over. But none of the major cultural and sports improvements would have been possible without the support of Lilly Endowment. Funded almost totally by Eli Lilly & Company stock, the endowment at one time was the largest in the nation. In the 1950s and 1960s, its managers favored supporting mostly evangelical Protestant churches and educational organizations in the U.S. and around the world. But by the 1970s the endowment leaders became convinced that the bulk of the grants should go to projects in the state and city if it hoped to attract world-class scientists and other brains. As a result, the endowment poured millions into education, sports complexes, and major capital improvements for a variety of cultural organizations—music, theater, dance, opera, art and museums.

The spending triggered an explosion of commercial ventures—hotels, restaurants, nightclubs and a $300 million shopping mall in the heart of downtown. The canal was cleaned up and winds through the impressive White River State Park. A zoo, new state museum, and a museum housing Indian and Western art, and new stadiums for professional baseball, basketball and football were built downtown. It became fashionable to live in the downtown area.

Throughout the transformation the public got involved. Thousands of residents volunteered to help carry out the National Sports Festival and the Pan Am Games. That overworked noun "community" took hold. When the Soldiers and Sailors Monument became "the world's largest Christmas tree" for the first time on Thanksgiving in 1962 fewer than a hundred people were there when the lights went on. Today the tree lighting attracts nearly 100,000. Similar numbers show up downtown for the fireworks display each Fourth of July, and the 500-Festival parade each May. The Festival's mini-marathon attracts 35,000 participants. Nearly 500,000 persons annually attend events staged at Indiana Black Expo, the largest black event of its kind in the nation.

7 • Where's Dog Town?

By mid-century Indianapolis had picked up a veneer of sophistication, not much, but enough to smooth some of its rougher edges.

Real estate developments carried such impressive names as Golden Hill, Windsor Village and Brendonwood—precursor to today's suburban developments with elegant British and French names, most of them trying to lure buyers with such pastoral suffixes as Forest, Field, Vale and Hills. If any justified such appellations, earth graders went to work to eliminate those attractions.

It was a different Indianapolis at the turn of the 20th century when neighborhood names fitted their locales. Names grew out of conditions that existed or people who lived there. The city was a patchwork of small areas, mostly poor and unattractive, with odd and colorful names. Dog Town evokes visions of hundreds of mangy dogs running loose on dirt streets, and that's the way it was in an area off of Bluff Road, some three miles south of Monument Circle.

Before the White River levee was built in 1913 the area along the river at 10th Street was called Pat Ward's Bottom, then later became The Levee. There was String Town and Straw Town, Storm Center and Little Italy, Irish Hill and Trader's Alley. Hooverville and Curtisville, south of Washington Street along White River, got their names during the Depression of the 1930s.

Few residents today can tell us the origins of the names of such neighborhoods as Love Town and The Valley, though Hunky Town probably reflected the influx of immigrants from Eastern Europe.

Many of the oddly named neighborhoods were in West Indianapolis. One of the neighborhoods still retains its name, at least for some of the older residents—Haughville, an area between 10th and Washington streets on Haugh Street and Pershing Avenue.

Tradition has it that Lost City, once located near the site of the Indiana University Medical Center, got its names because its houses rarely carried street numbers, and tenants knew each other only by their nicknames. Visitors were "lost" there if they didn't know their man as "Big Ear" or "Gate Mouth" or "Bad Eye." Some of the oldtimers on the police department at mid-century thought Lost City got its name from its mud-soaked streets and the absence of arc lights.

I can remember hearing about my Aunt Mary waking up one morning in Irish Hill and seeing a man impaled on the iron picket fence in front of the grocery store run by her father. Her family lived above the store. She was a young girl then so it must have happened around 1900. In those years the cops in Irish Hill kept busy on Friday nights breaking up fights that broke out after many of the laborers had spent a good part of their weekly wages in the taverns.

¤

8 • The Beginning

At mid-century *The Indianapolis News* was the dominant paper in Indiana. At its peak, *The News* had a circulation of 200,433. When it stopped publishing in 1999 its circulation had dropped to 34,000.

The News had been in business since 1869 when brash 23-year-old John Holliday founded it as an afternoon newspaper. Ironically, it folded because it was an afternoon paper, just one of hundreds of afternoon papers that eventually succumbed to television, lifestyle changes, and changing reader habits.

For most of the 20th century *The Star* and *The News* were the dominant papers in the state. Both got some spirited competition from the *Indianapolis Times*, a descendant of the old *Indianapolis Sun*, which was founded in 1888. The Scripps-Howard newspaper chain had bought the *Times* in 1922, but it gave up on October 11, 1965 because it was unable to compete for the advertising dollar and it, too, was beginning to feel the effects of television. Both *The Star* and *The News* hired many of the *Times* staffers.

George F. McCulloch of Muncie, who had made his fortune in the booming interurban business, began publishing *The Star* on June 6, 1903. To announce the paper's arrival, McCulloch paid a balloonist $650 to drop 500,000 red stars over the city for a week and also from atop the new Soldiers and Sailors Monument. I can confirm that the paper was selling for seven cents a week. I own a metal matchbox holder that mothers nailed on kitchen walls next to the gas stoves. It reads "1 cent daily, 1 cent Sunday" above the name, *The Indianapolis Morning Star*.

Indianapolis was a city of more than 170,000 when the first edition of The Star—a 12-pager—was published. *The Star* operated in a brick, eight-room Victorian residence at 115 East Ohio Street. It had been the home of the *Indianapolis Sun*. The paper took off in impressive fashion. After just six months its circulation reached 70,836.

Three months later *The Star* moved its editorial and arts departments, and the composing room force and pressmen, into the old *Sentinel* building in the first block of South Illinois Street. And six months later they moved again, this time to a four-story building on Monument Circle. When the *Sentinel* went out of business in 1906 after 65 years of publishing, *The Star* bought the *Sunday Sentinel*.

Finally, in 1907 *The Star* moved into a new, three-story brick building on the northeast corner of Pennsylvania and New York streets. It's been there ever since, though it has expanded many times. By then *The Star* was selling for 2 cents daily and 5 cents Sunday.

From its beginning *The Star* concentrated on local and state news. And from the start it was served by the Associated Press, a non-profit cooperative news service in which each member paper shares its reports with other member papers. *The Star* also subscribed to the United Press service, which was founded in 1902—60 years after AP had begun. In time UP merged with International News Service, a service started by William Randolph Hearst, and became UPI. Unlike AP, UPI sold its reports to papers. It went out of business in 1999.

On its first day of publication, an editorial proclaimed *The Star's* aim to be "an independent paper for the people—a newspaper, not an organ."

John C. Shaffer served as its publisher until he died in 1943. As late as the 1980s we were still receiving publicity releases addressed to Shaffer. A year after Shaffer died Pulliam bought the paper. Then on August 28, 1946, Pulliam bought *The News*, and two years later moved it from 30-32 West Washington Street to a building adjoining *The Star*. The papers were consolidated that year to reduce operating expenses, and all of the departments merged except for the two editorial departments. By then the city's population had grown to 400,000.

Members of the Fairbanks family had been the publishers of *The News*. Charles Warren Fairbanks, Vice-President under Theodore Roosevelt, assisted the paper financially but did not take part in publishing it. Pulliam always resented what he considered the patronizing attitude of the Fairbanks.

The Star and *The News* competed aggressively, though *Star* reporters and editors considered the *Times* the livelier competition. We considered *The News* soft, but it had several outstanding feature writers on both the city and sports staffs. *The News* staff—without justification, I might add—for many years treated *The Star* in a condescending manner.

But *The Star's* circulation continued to grow. By the end of the century it was printing 400,000 copies on Sunday and 230,000 daily while *The News* circulation dropped steadily year by year. To save money the editorial staffs of the two papers were combined in 1995. It didn't save *The News*. "The Great Hoosier Daily Since 1869" expired on October 1, 1999.

And in August 2000 the nation's largest newspaper chain, the Gannett Company, bought *The Star* and other papers controlled by the Pulliams.

9 • Climbing the Paper's Ladder

I was 24 when I started at *The Star* in November of 1949. I'd spent three years in the Army Air Corps (about half of that time in Brazil, SA) and three years at the University of Notre Dame where I obtained a degree in communication arts; the umbrella title which covered journalism, film, public relations and the like. The professors didn't emphasize reporting and newspaper writing, operating on the belief that we'd learn them on the job.

And I did learn on the job, wincing when an assistant city editor whittled my carefully crafted seven-inch story into three paragraphs. I soon noticed that other reporters got similar treatment. By the time a story cleared the copy desk and was sent to the composing room it might be penciled with deletions, corrections, new paragraphing, and topped with a headline written by a copy editor. But I learned, and looking back I think I progressed at the paper by a willingness to do any job assigned whether I liked it or not.

After 16 months on the police beat and a couple of years covering City Hall, I became an assistant city editor in late 1953 and was soon editing copy about as ruthlessly as had been done to my copy a year or so earlier. After seven years on the city desk I moved to the copy desk. I wasn't keen about working there but the six months I spent there taught me a lot. The training was invaluable when I became the slotman overseeing the work of all of the copy editors working around me on the horseshoe-shaped desk. There never seemed to be a free moment in that job. Except for an hour's break for dinner, I had my head buried in copy from 5 p.m. until 1 a.m.

I moved from the copy desk to become news editor in the summer of 1961. It was a major promotion. I was responsible for laying out page one and overseeing the stories and layout of all of the other pages in the paper.

By 1963 I had been working nights almost steadily for 14 years. The hours made life difficult for my wife Patty trying to take care of our young children who arrived almost yearly. I decided I'd better get out of the business and get a day job somewhere, and also earn more money, so I told Bob Early of my decision. That's when he divulged that Lowell Parker, the city editor, was going to be leaving to become managing editor of the *Phoenix Gazette.* Would I like to replace him? Early even suggested that I work from 10 a.m. to 7 p.m., rather than the 1:30 p.m. to 11 p.m. hours that Lowell had been working.

It solved our problem, sort of. The day hours pleased Patty, but she

Bo Connor rear (l-r), Patty, Carrie, Julie; front (l-r)Janet, Michael, Maureen, Larry about 1966.

regularly insisted that the job came first with me, the family second. I always disagreed but there were times when it seemed so. A city editor's life is dictated by the day's events. You don't walk away from a breaking story. But the new job and the new hours eased my conscience and it enabled me to be at home at night to help with the children, who were soon to number six. Without Patty's understanding and forbearance I would never have lasted at the paper.

I spent 16 years as city editor, a grueling job. Some nights I would leave the office amazed at the amount of work I had done that day. I felt like a phone had been fused on my ear keeping in touch with reporters and fielding calls from the public and, of course, the managing editor. I was aided by an assistant city editor, who came in at 1:30 p.m. to begin editing both daily and Sunday copy, and taking phone calls, and by the night city editor who arrived at 5 p.m.

At the risk of appearing self-important, I viewed the job as a vocation. And I felt, too, that all of us, including the publisher, were simply the paper's stewards; that the paper belonged to the community. But I didn't fool myself that many staff members would have bought into my views had I made them public.

Relief from the pressures of the city editor's job came in 1979 when Frank Crane, the editor of the editorial page, retired. Gene Pulliam asked me to take his place. The pace was much slower and I was able to write an occasional column or turn out an editorial advising the White House on some major issue. I loved that job, but it lasted only three months before Bob Early decided to retire. He was 74 and had been managing editor for 34 years. Gene offered me the job and I quickly accepted. John H. (Jerry) Lyst, who had been business editor for 12 years, then replaced me as editor.

Early had always worked late at night and often into early morning, but I chose to work from 9 a. m. to 6 p. m., though the day actually began about 8 o'clock when I'd show up at Shapiro's restaurant on South Meridian Street where I'd order a pastry and coffee and go through the paper page by page looking for items to criticize or commend. I really wasn't finished at 6 in the evening, either. At 10 o'clock every night a cab would pull up to the house with a copy of the bulldog edition. I'd go through it rapidly and then call the news editor to ask about the latest news and offering corrections, most of them already caught by the copy desk.

I'd seen all kinds of reporters in the years I spent at the paper. I learned that it wasn't only the journalism school graduate who made the best reporter; some of our best ones had only high school educations, but they were the kinds of reporters who had learned well on the job, became self-educated, read voraciously, and had natural curiosity.

The ideal reporter would be energetic, curious, honest, thorough, persistent, egocentric, imaginative, resourceful, opinionated, fair, decent, loyal, dedicated, uncompromising, principled, tactful, and tasteful in dress and demeanor. And probably dull, too.

On a practical level, it would be ideal to build a staff with a mix of individuals in sex, age and race, one that had individuals with a mix of social, educational, economic, religious and even geographic backgrounds, a mix that would enable the paper to reflect the interests of the total community. There is a hazard that a staff of elitists—affluent and educated persons with upper middle-class values and interests—would have trouble relating to the welder, the coal miner, the short-order cook.

I sometimes deliberately drove through different neighborhoods, especially the poorer areas, to get a rough idea of them. And I was convinced that if a reporter went to a party, he or she could pick up ideas for two or three stories just by being alert.

We had all types of people covering the news—extroverts and introverts, liberals and conservatives, self-starters and those who had to be guided and motivated and shoved. Some were in it for the excitement; some for the satisfaction it provided. But to many it was just a job. We lost many talented people who didn't see a future in a job that promised a $5 weekly merit raise once a year. They moved on, often into public relations. Some became successful business executives and some credited their journalism background as one of the reasons they had succeeded.

I worried sometimes that the editorial department was top heavy with Catholics. Most of the key editorial jobs were held by Catholics. I was unable to ask an applicant about his religion, but I could usually tell during the interview. One day I hired Graham LeStourgeon. He'd been working for the Volunteers of America but he had a background in journalism. I saw him as a good, dependable reporter—and Protestant, too. A few months later, though, I learned that Graham had converted to Catholicism. He later returned to his work with Volunteers of America in Columbus, Ohio.

Frustration in the newsroom was a byproduct of the business. So many things can go wrong. The tip on a story falls through after four hours running it down. A story needs to be rewritten. The phones rarely stop ringing. Public relations specialists show up to tout their clients, and visitors drift in with some hare-brained ideas for a story.

The rush to put out a newspaper every day often produced ulcers, alcoholism, lung cancer, stress, depression, and headaches, but there was always that euphoria when a major story broke. I never quite forgot what it was like to hear and feel the presses rumble in the basement at 9:30 at night when the bulldog edition would begin its run. A few minutes later one of the copy boys would come in from the mailroom with an armload of papers; the ink still not completely dry. We'd grab a copy to see how well —or poorly—we had performed.

Technology has altered much of the business. The first to go were the stereotypers, then computers wiped out the linotype operators and most of the printers, and the work of engravers and photo lab jobs have been rendered obsolete by digital cameras. The presses still rumble but not at 307 North Pennsylvania Street. They rumble in spacious and pristine quarters 15 miles from the newsroom. The pressmen seldom get dirty. I wonder if they still wear those hats they made from newspapers.

¤

10 • A Patrician Gentlemen

Gene Pulliam may have owned the papers, but Bill Dyer ran them. Little escaped him, especially if it concerned amassing and spending money. Tall and broad-shouldered, he was intelligent and shrewd, patrician and courtly in manner. He rarely raised his voice and always appeared to be in control. He treated all of the 1,700 employees with respect—and it usually paid off when the craft unions sat down to negotiate new contracts.

Pulliam hired William A. Dyer, Jr. in 1944 to run *The Star* with the title vice-president and general manager, and when he bought *The News* four years later Dyer became vice-president and general manager of both papers. He was named president of Indianapolis Newspapers Inc. in 1975.

Dyer had hoped to become a drama critic after graduating from Brown University in 1924, but when the *Syracuse* (NY) *Journal* hired him it was to sell advertising. He later moved to the *Syracuse Post-Standard* where he became director of general advertising. Both in Syracuse and in Indianapolis Dyer became a community leader with special interest in the arts.

There was little in the organization—advertising, circulation, editorial and production—that escaped Bill Dyer's notice. Not one to pioneer, he usually waited until the wrinkles in new technologies had been ironed out on other papers before adopting them.

After I became managing editor I had to prepare an annual budget of some $9 million. I always felt we were understaffed and underfunded, and so my proposed budget was designed to rectify the shortages. I assumed that other department heads were taking similar steps. But each year when all of us were called to defend our budgets, we could count on Bill Dyer warning us that the year ahead was going to be difficult. If it wasn't a shaky economy, an expected increase in the cost of newsprint was reason enough for alarm, we'd be warned. The year ending may have turned out to have been a good one financially, but next year promised to be grim, so let's start trimming those requests.

There were days when reporters were told to turn in the stubs of pencils before getting new ones. If reporters wanted to take notes in spiral notebooks, they had to buy them. Most reporters left on assignment with sheets of 8-by-11 newsprint folded into thirds.

When Dyer became an octogenarian, he would nod off at the department head meetings held after a martini-fueled lunch on Wednesday afternoons, but when the subject of spending came up, he came alive.

Editors across the country were beginning to notice that reporters and editors who spent long periods on computer keyboards were reporting pains in their wrists. It was the first reports of the carpal tunnel syndrome. When some staff members complained to me about sore wrists, I thought the power of suggestion was at work. But more and more of them claimed to be affected. How many copy editors were genuinely injured or were just imagining pain was difficult to tell, but it was an issue we had to deal with. After we called in some work-place engineers, they informed us that we needed to replace most of the desks and chairs to eliminate the risks for the staff.

I made a mistake of not informing Dyer of the problem before we brought in the engineers. When we requisitioned several thousand dollars to purchase the desks and chairs, he became angry. He said that if the editorial department came up with new equipment, other departments would demand similar improvements. We finally got the furniture and fears of rampant spending in other departments never materialized. In fact, most of the departments had been well ahead of the editorial department in refurbishing their quarters.

The cost of newsprint was always a consideration, so each day the editorial department was allotted so much space for news and features. If a major news story broke or the sports department needed more space than it was allotted that day, we would inform the person dummying the paper with display advertising about our needs. Usually, we'd get the extra space reluctantly after the man dummying the paper would groan about it. He knew that he would be called on to justify his reasons for increasing the editorial space in the paper, especially if it meant adding pages to the paper.

We always had to make a case for large amounts of additional space over the next few days for some series that one of our investigative teams had written. These lengthy series seemed to irritate Bill Dyer. He questioned whether readers would bother to plow through a full page of stories and photos and charts. He felt that we had our eye on some journalism prize when we came up with those series. With a bit of give and take, though, we'd usually get enough space to run the series.

But when he heard that we were requesting extra space to run a lengthy series on cancer, he became distressed for another reason. He insisted that subscribers would be unhappy reading about the subject. Killing or drastically trimming a series that four or five reporters had worked on for weeks would cause a major morale problem in the newsroom, so three of us requested a meeting. The city editor, Dennis Royalty, and the project director made the case for running the series. It was an important topic and the stories were almost impassioned. Dyer finally disclosed that one of his concerns would be the stress it would place on cancer victims, one of whom was his wife, who had undergone successful cancer treatment a few months earlier.

After making our case, he finally threw up his hands and snapped, "Go ahead and run it and win another prize."

I've forgotten how many prizes we won for the series, but I know it convinced a lot of readers to stop smoking, including me.

¤

11 • The Cop Shop

Most cub reporters at the paper underwent an unscripted indoctrination period. It could last a month or up to six months. Their duties included writing obituaries, rewriting public relations blurbs, and doing whatever menial tasks desk editors ordered. After their brief introduction to journalism, they became police reporters. They may have had dreams of being a columnist or covering politics, but they had to put those dreams on hold and spend days and nights working out of the dingy pressroom at police headquarters.

The police beat was important because *The Star* devoted a lot of space to crime, accidents and fires. But it was even more important for new reporters (almost totally males) because it gave them a broader education on human behavior than they had been getting in college dorms. It taught them about the location and living conditions in diverse neighborhoods. It taught them how to get along with policemen and firemen, lawyers and judges, and emergency room doctors and nurses. And it taught them how to gather facts quickly and accurately.

A few of the reporters never learned to stand up to some of the more arrogant cops to gather information. If they let the cops intimidate them, they didn't last long on the beat. Police reporters rarely wrote stories; they phoned their notes to a rewriteman. Novice reporters learned quickly that every name had to include a middle initial, that all addresses had to be exact, and the information complete or they could expect to be sent back to get more details.

Some police reporters spent years on the beat; others lasted only a few weeks. Some loved the work; others soon tired of it, or felt that perhaps a job in public relations might be more lucrative. It usually was.

One of the better police reporters was Bill Scifres. He had become a veteran police reporter but one day told the city editor, Lowell Parker, that he had to get off the beat. He said he could no longer go on runs in which a child was the victim. In time, he became the makeup editor in the composing room and wrote an outdoor column for the sports department.

Police reporters may have undergone stretches of boredom lounging in the pressroom waiting for the police radio to bark out the location of some local calamity, but a few months chasing cops around Indianapolis was invaluable in introducing reporters to the exciting and glamorous world of journalism portrayed on *Law and Order* and *NYPD Blues*. Well, maybe not quite that exciting, or that glamorous.

The Star's police reporters spent less time on the beat than those on *The*

News or the *Times*. Mac Trusnik, a longtime police reporter for *The News*, kept a running list of all of the reporters who had worked the police beat in the 41 years (April 1953 to January 1994) he had been covering the police beat. His list contained the names of 100 *Star* reporters, 39 *News* reporters, and 28 *Times* reporters who had worked there until their paper folded in October 1965.

Generally *The News* preferred assigning reporters on its different beats for years, figuring that the reporters got to know the sources so well that they would rarely be scooped. It wasn't our policy. Leaving reporters on a beat too long would make them bored, careless, or lazy, or so we reasoned, while a fresh reporter would be eager with a different outlook.

One exception was Bill Anderson who covered the police beat off and on for 30 years or more. He loved the excitement it promised and often delivered. His contacts in the department were invaluable when he teamed with two other reporters to conduct a six-month investigation of corruption in the Indianapolis Police Department, an investigation that brought the paper its first Pulitzer Prize in 1974.

Bill always found some redeeming feature in everyone. "Aw, he's a good guy," Bill would counter when a co-worker might be referring to a policeman as a "crooked son of a bitch." But that outlook didn't stop him from opposing anyone who dared to interfere with his reporting.

When Craig Ito, a recent Butler University graduate, was assigned to the police beat, he was introduced to some of the cops by the police reporter he was replacing. The pair walked into the chief's office and Craig was introduced to the chief, Dan Veza, a big, friendly Italian-American. Dan rose from his chair, bowed formally and said very slowly, "So nice to meet you."

When they left the office, Craig, born in the U. S., shook his head and said, "What's with him?"

It wasn't the only occasion when his Japanese heritage was noted. In time Craig moved on to the copy desk where some of his co-workers liked to rib him about practicing "yellow" journalism. One of his friends on the desk, Dennis Hoffman, said he was awakened early one December morning when he got a call from Craig, who was vacationing in Seattle. "Happy Pearl Harbor Day, Dennis," Craig said.

When I began my 16 months on the police beat in the winter of 1950, I worked the 6 p.m. to 2 a.m. shift and so had little direct competition from reporters on *The News* and the *Times* because they worked the daytime shifts. On nights when the citizens were behaving, I'd sit in the cramped pressroom under the stairs in the old police headquarters on Alabama Street waiting for something to happen. I'd check the police reports or wander across Alabama Street to the county jail and the sheriff's office.

The pressroom was a few feet from the main entrance to the ancient building. It was about six feet by 12 feet, just large enough to hold three old wooden desks, each with a telephone for the three newspapers. The sloping ceiling was the bottom side of a stairway. There was no space for radio reporters, and television was in the future. Now and then a reporter from one of the radio stations would rush into the building, shove a microphone at the police chief or homicide captain for a one-line comment and rush out.

There were nights when I never left to go on a run, but I could usually count on someone dropping by to keep me company. John Hannon, a deputy prosecutor working the night shift, was a regular when he wasn't processing some miscreant upstairs. Sometimes a cop would pop in after his shift ended. Now and then it would be one of the sleazy hangers-on at headquarters.

For several years Horace Ketring and Heze Clark worked against each other during the day shift, Horace for *The News*, and Heze for the *Times*.

The story goes that Horace knew that Heze was working on a scoop one morning but didn't know what it was all about. Both had direct lines to their city desks so they could dictate their notes and stories to rewritemen. Their desks abutted and their phones sat next to each other. When Heze stepped out of the pressroom briefly, Horace switched the phones. Guarding his scoop, Heze carefully whispered the details of his exclusive to what he thought was the *Times* city desk. Alerted to Ketring's ploy, a rewriteman for *The News* quietly took the information from Heze. His scoop made page one of *The News*, and Heze was dismayed that he couldn't find his story in the *Times*.

Clark, an aging, burly ex-coach and athlete, followed an unchanging routine when phoning information to the rewrite desk. He would quote verbatim from the police report, beginning with the time that the call first came in, which cars were dispatched to the scene, the names of the officers involved and eventually he'd get around to providing details of the story. If a rewriteman dared to break in and ask, "Heze, what's it all about?" Heze would simply cut him off and begin again, "Police were called at 6:15 a.m. to a house at so-and-so." The *Times* deskmen learned it was best to bear with him.

It was exciting to race to the scene of some major accident or crime hanging on to Emergency Car 5, a huge, open-air wagon that was almost a mini police station. It carried first aid experts and it also carried machine guns, rifles, sawed-off shotguns, tear gas, wrenches, pry bars, fire extinguishers, stretchers, splints, blankets, gas masks, spotlights, grappling hooks, a Chemox machine to determine the kind and extent of gas in a contaminated room, and two resuscitators. The cops didn't usually object when a reporter jumped on the wagon as it was pulling out of headquarters. Fire department rescue teams later replaced the ancient wagon.

Usually, though, we'd use the paper's staff car to drive to the scene. Each of us had to haul along the bulky Speed Graphic camera along with a bag of film and flashbulbs. "Did you get any art?" was usually the deskman's first question. I can't remember ever having one of my photos used in the paper. I never mastered the damned thing, usually forgetting one of the steps in getting the camera loaded or forgetting to install a flash bulb. And I didn't want to fool with it while I was trying to gather information.

My cousin, Jim Connor, spent a shift with me one night. His deceased father (my Uncle Harry) had been a detective on the force. Jim watched as I went through the police reports, and made some phone calls to various departments. All very routine and dull. Then over the police radio we heard the dispatcher send a police car and an ambulance to an intersection on Shelby Street where a boy was hit by a motorcycle. Jim and I raced to the location. It was a gruesome scene. Part of the boy's brain was on the pavement. I called the city desk to report what had happened and was directed to go to the boy's home to get information about him and to ask for his picture, always a ticklish business. The man who answered the door was the boy's father, though at first we did not know that. He said he had heard something about his son being in an accident and asked, "Is it bad?" Just as I answered that his son was dead, Jim, trying to soften the blow, blurted, "He's hurt real bad."

Back at the pressroom I gave the information to a rewriteman, and then we headed to 25th Street and Northwestern Avenue to check on another report of a man hit by a car. This one was even grimmer. While I was talking to a policeman, Jim stuck his head under the front of the car that had been jacked up. He was looking at a battered skull. The victim had ended up in a sitting position under the car with his head in the motor.

It was enough for Jim. He headed home and never accompanied me again, though he later became an attorney and spent many hours in the courtrooms in the City-County Building.

In those years before race riots and civil rights dominated the news, we paid very little attention to blacks in the city. They lived in mostly slum neighborhoods, many of them living in shanties, some even without indoor plumbing. It was common at headquarters to read a police report about a black person's body floating in the Indianapolis Water Company canal that ran along the west side of downtown. Those reports of bodies in the canal rarely made the paper. In fact, the first question asked by the desk editor when I called about a possible story was, "Is it black?" If so, the response would be, "Forget it."

It was several years before that cavalier treatment changed in the city and at the paper. The Civil Rights Act of 1964 altered a lot of thinking. We hired our first black reporter about that time and in subsequent years added several more as reporters, editors, and photographers. Stories featuring African-American subjects regularly appear in the paper today.

Sometimes it takes patience to get a story. I noticed that each year the National Safety Council rated Indianapolis's streets one of the safest in the nation. So on a slow day I interviewed Captain Audry Jacobs, who had been in charge of the traffic division for several years. We pored over charts and statistics for an hour or so, but it didn't promise much of a story. But as I was getting ready to leave, I asked him why he had become so interested in traffic safety.

When he was a boy, he said, he saw his father driving home a team of horses hauling a load of hay. He said two young hotrodders racing down the country road hit the wagon, killing his dad. "That's why I've always been interested in accident prevention," he said.

That throwaway question turned what promised to be a routine statistical account into a decent human interest feature story.

Another routine question produced an unusual angle on a story about a shooting in Rome, Indiana, late one night. Rome was a remote town of 40 souls or so on the Ohio River. I was able to get the town's telephone operator on the line.

"Know anything about a shooting there?" I asked.

"Sure," she said. "I can see it right out the front window." And then she described what had been happening.

"Do you know the guy doing the shooting?" I asked.

"Oh yes," she said.

"Anything unusual about him?"

"Well," she said, "he's had this habit of walking around town with a pillow on his back. Afraid someone would shoot him."

The telephone is a handy tool for reporters.

Carl Henn, who was working on the rewrite desk on the *Times,* heard the report of a fire on the police radio on the city desk. While the police reporter was driving to the scene, Carl checked the crisscross directory, which listed phone numbers by addresses. He picked a number and made a call hoping to find someone living in the vicinity of the fire. A man answered and Carl said he was calling from the *Times* and asked:

"Is there a fire around there?"

"Yes," the man said.

"Where is it?" Henn asked.

"It's right here," he answered.

"Well, what are you doing?" Carl asked.

"I'm answering the phone," he replied, then said apologetically, "I've got to leave now."

One of the paper's street sales hawkers became the subject of a story herself one night. Her name was Dortha L. Hunter. She sold copies of the first edition (the bulldog) on Monument Circle each night. At other hours she could be seen feeding the pigeons in University Park. The police tagged her "Pigeon Woman." They arrested her several times as a public nuisance, but newspaper street vendors were hard to find, so Dortha always kept her job.

One night there was a run to a house in the 3200 block of Ruckle Street on report of a woman found dead in an upstairs bedroom. I drove to the house. It was Dortha. She had been dead for two days. No foul play involved, but the house made the story. It looked like it had been abandoned. The living room held only an aged upright piano. A couch without cushions sat in the dining room, along with a round table covered with aged newspapers that had become glued to the surface, a stove in the kitchen with a clothes iron and a vacuum sweeper. Except for her bedroom, the rest of the house was bare. When I entered, a 14-inch crow and two pigeons were perched on top of the door in the front room. Bird feed and bird waste littered the floor.

I went upstairs to the bedroom. The old woman was in a blood-smeared bed. When the coroner and a policeman rolled her over, she was stiff. I had to leave.

Dortha wasn't our only odd newspaper hawker. Beep Beep pulled his papers in a little red wagon. He yelled at customers, especially women. Beep Beep had a goatee and was always filthy. He was still pulling the wagon and yelling up until he died at the age of 90.

Another one showed up regularly sporting a bandage. One week he might have an arm in a sling, and the next week it would be the other arm. Sometimes he bandaged his hand or a placed a patch over his eye. We surmised he thought it would induce people to buy a paper out of pity.

Over the years Indianapolis had amassed an arcane collection of crimes on its books. You could be fined $100 if you urged a pair of dogs to fight. If a woman's hatpin extended out more than a half inch, she was subject to a $5 fine. Hypnotists were subject to arrest if they kept a victim under their spell for more than an hour. Throwing dry ice on streets was forbidden, as was keeping chickens in the city, or tossing stones across streets or alleys. Had to keep the kids in line.

Of course these "crimes" were ignored, but not bingo games, high stakes poker, pea-shake houses and slot machines in private clubs and lodges, and houses of prostitution. The raids on these dens of iniquity were mostly pro forma. The police were demonstrating that Indianapolis did not tolerate sin. The professional gamblers and the madams at the whorehouses went along with the program. They paid their fines and then resumed business.

Then in the 1990s gambling no longer was a crime; it became a major source of income for the state. After the legislature and the governor approved the lottery, it wasn't long before the state got riverboat casinos, licensed bingo games, pari-mutuel racing and off-track betting. Suddenly, puritanical Indiana was outdoing Nevada.

¤

12 • A Likeable Scoundrel

After 16 months on the police beat, I became the City Hall reporter in 1952. I roamed the marble halls and sat in on meetings of the various boards that ran the city—public safety, public works, parks, health, zoning and planning. My mother was a member of the park board and the planning commission, but she was never good for a scoop. When I wasn't dozing at a board meeting, I was trudging up and down the stairs in that impressive building several hours each day, going from one office to another seeking whatever news I could pick up.

I'd check in about once a week with the director of public health, Dr. Henry G. Nester, who held that post from 1952 to 1970. Tall, slow talking, he never seemed to be busy. Whenever I asked, "What's going on?" he invariably embarked on a lecture about the city's need to control rabies. None of the other diseases under his umbrella got mentioned. I never understood his concern because the incidence of rabies was miniscule. After finishing his rabies lecture, he'd suggest that I talk to the rat control officer, a young man who was enthusiastic about his war against the varmints. I would listen as he explained where rats could be found and how he exterminated them. The rats, he admitted, always got ahead of him.

Since rats, especially photos of rats, were one of the paper's taboos, I really was wasting my time with him because the paper wasn't interested in running stories about the vile creatures.

Covering City Hall gave me my first contact with wily politicians. In dealing with the press, they tend to appear thoughtful and put on guarded fronts. They respond to questions with the standard bromides—"Let me just say"... "That's a good question"... "I'm glad you asked that"—followed by a blah answer or a glib switch to a subject that was self-serving or vapid.

One exception was Alex M. Clark, who was mayor when I was covering City Hall. A Municipal Court judge, he was elected in 1951 and served one term before he returned to the practice of law. I would have described him as a likeable scoundrel. There was no pretense with Alex.

Shortly after he became mayor, he replaced the previous Democrat-controlled board of sanitation with one controlled by Republicans. One of the new board's first acts was to authorize a $75,000 contract to an engineering consulting firm to study the city's sewer needs. It made no difference to Alex that the previous board had completed and paid for a similar study. The contract (lucrative for those years) went to a friend of the new board president.

It was just the sort of political chicanery that Ted Knap relished exposing. Ted was a hotshot political reporter for the *Indianapolis Times.* He showed up at City Hall one summer morning to fill in for a few days for the vacationing reporter who regularly covered the beat.

If news was scarce, Ted found ways to come up with stories.

He came to City Hall that first day with a page one story that had "heated" Democrats questioning the need for another sewer contract.

After a couple of days of page one stories in the *Times* about this "unconscionable" waste of taxpayers' money, the mayor reacted in standard fashion. He named a non-partisan committee of businessmen to investigate the dispute. To safeguard the committee members from pressure, Alex said he chose to keep their names secret. But Ted got what he wanted —another page one story; this one about formation of the committee with instructions from the mayor to "let the chips fall where they may."

Knap returned to his regular duties at the *Times* when the City Hall reporter returned from his two-week vacation, but it didn't stop Ted from periodically calling the mayor to ask about the committee's findings, and Clark kept saying they needed more time.

Finally, Clark told Knap that the committee had made its report and decided that the contract was "OK."

"That's not what I heard," Ted said. "One of my sources called and said he thinks the city is getting a raw deal."

"Is that so?" the mayor said. "Who was it?"

"I can't tell you," Knap said.

A few weeks later, I asked the mayor, "Whatever happened with that committee?" Alex grinned and said, "Keep this to yourself, but I never did appoint a committee."

On another occasion some scandal erupted in his administration. And this one elicited interest from reporters at all three of the local papers. After being badgered daily by the reporters about the latest developments, Clark told the trio of City Hall reporters that the constant questioning was taking far too much of his time. So he told the reporters that he would answer just one question from each of them in private. *The Star's* reporter at that time was Donald Ruby. He let the reporters from the *Times* and *The News* have their turn in the mayor's office before he confronted the mayor.

"OK, Don, what's your question?" Alex asked. Conscious of not being scooped, Don answered, "What did you tell those guys?"

Both Ted and Don later moved on to Washington, Ted as Washington correspondent for Scripps-Howard, the chain that owned the *Times*, and Don as administrative aide to Congressman Richard Roudebush.

One of the young reporters who came to *The Star* from the *Times* after it folded in 1965 also ended up in Washington. One afternoon he came into the city room excited about an exclusive story involving shenanigans by a well-respected real estate executive. The story seemed to have promise until I asked what the executive had to say about the charges.

"Oh, I didn't ask him," he said. "If you ask too many questions, you lose a good story."

"Go see him," I said.

An hour later he was back, confessing that "there's no story."

I should have fired him but we rarely fired anyone. He didn't stay long, though. He left to take a job in Washington—appropriately with the United States Information Agency.

¤

13 • The Press Under Attack

There is everywhere an increasingly angry disillusionment about the press, a growing sense of being baffled and misled; and wise publishers will not pooh-pooh these omens.... If publishers and authors themselves do not face the facts and attempt to deal with them, some day Congress, in a fit of temper, egged on by an outraged public opinion, will operate on the press with an ax.

It's a warning heard frequently, but this one was issued in 1920 by the nation's foremost journalist and author, Walter Lippmann.

The press always has been a target for unhappy readers and listeners. Plagiarism, the use of anonymous sources, and biased reporting are current concerns of editors. There are watchdog readers ready to pounce if they spot any sin. At almost any convention of editors you can expect a panel on ethics. The irony in all of this is that the press today is far more diligent about its conduct than in the past. Free trips, free passes, gifts from public relations practitioners and a bottle of whiskey from the police property room at Christmas—all common perks in newsrooms a half century ago—are now prohibited in most newsrooms. I don't ever remember any pay-back with favorable stories. The press wasn't so full of itself in those days, but after a few years the publisher decided it was time to stop the practice of accepting gifts.

Even with the best of intentions, newspapers can get it wrong. Each day an imperfect and incomplete and simplified version of some of what went on fills the pages. A newspaper seeks out the events and happenings that are of the most interest to the largest number of readers, and it isn't always the most important events. Sometimes the messages have no real significance; they merely amuse or entertain or divert the reader. But often when readers don't like what they're reading they go after the messenger.

Certainly the major events in the nation and the world are covered and analyzed, but the news that excites and stimulates reporters and editors, and readers, too, are society's aberrations—scandals, tragedies, heroics, wars, cataclysmic events. News is a deviation from the norm. Because editors look for news and stories that will interest the greatest number of readers, the scandal or crime or violent act often gets prominent play. Journalism lives off the sins and mistakes of humans. People who behave make good citizens; they rarely make news.

Gee Whiz was operating in the business a half century ago when I was a cub reporter and it still operates today. We liked to deal in superlatives—the tallest, longest, shortest, oldest, youngest, newest, biggest, smallest, first, last. A few stories may have some lasting historic value, but generally the paper is designed to be read in an hour or two and cast aside until the next day's edition arrives.

Some readers criticize the paper for failing to be something it was never intended to be. They ask, "Why doesn't the paper record more of the good deeds? Why isn't it more literary, more Christian? Why doesn't it try to educate the masses?"

Newspapers sometimes do manage to uplift and guide but those are byproducts of the paper's attempt to reflect what's going on in the world. If papers set out to be altruistic, they would negate their proper role of informing their readers. In countries where the government controls the press, readers get guidance, but they don't get news.

In truth, most of the space in a newspaper has always been filled with the good news, or at least neutral information—sports, how-to and advice columns, fashions, entertainment, comics, human interest features and pictures, business data, lists of upcoming events, and reports of who was born, married, divorced, promoted, sued, honored and died. But the bad news—the news that reports what went wrong—is what fascinates most readers. It's what they turn to first, the news they remember and discuss with their neighbors and friends, the news that makes them ask the age-old question—"What's wrong with the world today?" But read it they must. If all stories were sugarcoated, they might some day wake up to find that the barbarians had returned and they'll cry out:

"Why didn't the papers tell us what was going on?"

¤

14 • A Wronged Woman Retaliates

Newspapers thrive on scandal. A juicy scandal energizes the staff. And when it happens in mid-summer when news is scarce, it's especially welcome. It may seem crass and not the sort of admission a journalist should be making, but a ripe scandal is certainly more interesting to cover than a city council hearing on next year's budget.

And that's why *The Star* and its readers couldn't get enough of the Connie Nicholas-Forrest Teel affair in the summer of 1958. When Connie put three bullets into Forrest shortly after midnight on July 31, there were enough angles in their lives together to keep the story on page one for weeks. Even rabid fans of the soap operas that dominated daytime television left their beds early each morning to read about the latest developments in the city's real-life soap opera.

The victim was 54 years old, a handsome, socially prominent executive of Eli Lilly & Co. at that time the world's largest pharmaceutical manufacturer. And, not surprisingly, the paper's number one sacred cow.

The killer was a middle-age divorcee who had been the victim's lover for 15 years, but at the age of 44 discovered that she was being jilted for an attractive 29-year-old secretary at Lilly's.

When the police dispatcher sent a car to investigate a report of a shooting outside the Meadowbrook apartments on East 38th Street that early morning, *The Star's* police reporter, Don Ruby, went along. Young professionals and office workers and newly married couples favored the apartment complex on the northside. It was a crime-free area at that time, so the call held promise of a story. Don knew he didn't have much time because the paper's final edition deadline was fast approaching.

When he called the city desk a few minutes after he arrived, he was excited. He said the victim was a well-dressed man wearing a blue summer suit. The cops found him slumped over the steering wheel of a white, late-model Cadillac sedan. He said an onlooker volunteered to the police that he was "some sort of a big shot at Lilly's" and his name was Forrest Teel. We knew then we were on to a big story. Don hounded the police and onlookers for as much information as he could gather, while back at the city room reporters began tracking down public relations sources at Lilly. Our library, called the morgue in those years, came up with a biographical sketch and photograph of Teel.

Don began feeding information to the rewriteman. He said that a policeman pulled Teel upright from the steering wheel, and that his head was moving from side to side as though he was having trouble breathing.

When the cops asked him what happened, who had shot him, Teel shook his head, moaning repeatedly, "Get me to a hospital." But he died at the scene about 15 minutes later. It was just past 1 o'clock in the morning.

The news editor held back the page-one deadline enough to give us time to get an adequate, though incomplete, story and photo of Teel as the lead story on the page. At that hour no one knew who had shot him and why.

Forrest Teel

Forrest Teel was a success by society's standards. Tall, slim, and handsome, he was executive vice-president of marketing at Lilly and president of Eli Lilly International, and had just recently had been named to the company's board of directors. He was on the fast track. He was fluent in three languages and had spent several years with the company in Latin America. Some friends and co-workers described him as bright and charming. Others thought him arrogant and pompous. Lilly's unwritten dress code was conservative suits, white shirts and modest ties. Its employees were expected to do minimal drinking and avoid the limelight. Teel's murder and extracurricular activities brought shock and shame to Lilly's boardroom.

Teel had been married to the former Mary Elizabeth (Betty) Roddy for 26 years. They had an adopted son who was then 14. Betty Teel was a small, shy, attractive woman who was dominated by a demanding and uncaring husband. They lived in one of the city's posh neighborhoods. He flew his own new Cessna airplane, and was considered a good country club golfer.

The morning after the shooting police got a tip from a pawnbroker that they should be looking for a woman named Connie Nicholas. He said she had purchased a 25-caliber pistol from his shop a couple of weeks earlier and had talked him into giving her four free lessons on a target range.

The police went to Connie's apartment in Marcy Village, another upscale apartment complex on the city's northside, but no one answered. Instead they found taped to the front door a key and a suicide note. Inside the spotless apartment they found other suicide notes and instructions to return a pair of slippers and a bathrobe to Teel's home at 5921 Washington Boulevard. They also found some unmailed letters, two of them addressed to Teel.

The police located Connie that evening in her blue Chevrolet in a wooded area off of Fall Creek Parkway near 46th Street, an area sometimes used as a lover's lane. Tall oak and pine trees hid the car that was mired in mud. Wearing a fashionable pink dress, she was in the driver's seat facing the passenger door with both of her legs tucked under her and both hands and her head resting on top of the seat. She was unconscious. A thermos and two red capsules were on the seat beside her. There was evidence that she had vomited, and that she had been crying. In her purse was a newspaper photo of Teel, a gun and seven bullets.

She was taken to General Hospital where she remained comatose through most of the next day. She had mashed more than 75 prescription sleeping pills, mixed them with pineapple juice, and drank the mixture. Physicians estimated that she had ingested the mixture around noontime, some eight hours before she was discovered. Ironically, the pills were made by Lilly and given to her by Teel.

While Connie lay comatose, an autopsy performed on Teel showed that he had been shot three times; once in the neck, hip, and abdomen.

When Connie came out of the coma, the first thing she asked was "How is Forrest?" She sobbed when told that he had died. She admitted shooting him but said it was an accident. Reporters were camped at the hospital, but she refused to talk to any of them. On the third day, though, she relented and some 20 reporters and photographers crowded around her bed. They discovered that Connie was a talker, alternately sobbing and talking about her clandestine relationship with Teel.

She said that she had been having an affair with him for 15 years. During that time, she said, Teel and his wife had adopted a son. And she said that she had been married and divorced twice. She told of taking trips with Teel. She said they had an agreement that they would marry after his son completed high school and he had obtained a divorce. Three weeks earlier, when she learned that Teel had a new girl friend, she said that she began following him in her car. He stopped his car once, got out and angrily told her she had to stop following him, she said.

When she learned that the woman he was seeing was a secretary at Lilly's named Laura Mowrer, she drove to the Meadowbrook apartment complex where she lived. She saw Teel's Cadillac parked outside and waited in it for three hours until he came out of the building shortly before 1 a. m. They argued and he struck her, she said, and threw her across the seat. It didn't require much effort because Connie was tiny—5-foot, 1-inch and 105 pounds. She said during the struggle that the gun she was carrying went off three times. While they were struggling, Teel backed up his car and it slammed into a utility pole. As he slumped over the steering wheel, Connie said she got out of his car and drove off in her 3-year-old blue Chevrolet.

The Star's reporter interviewing Connie in the hospital was Phil Clifford, a dapper gentleman who always wore a neatly pressed suit and tie. When he returned to the city room he said Connie had sobbed a lot during the interview and had cried out, "I love him. I love him. I love him." After he wrote a vivid account of the interview, he got a call from the city editor of the *New York Daily News*, a paper that he had been stringing for regularly. The paper asked for the story and Phil got an OK from his city editor, Lowell Parker, to wire the story he had written. They liked the story so much that the *Daily News* managing editor offered him $250. It was probably twice as much as Phil's weekly salary. He was feeling pretty good about the bonus until he got another call, this one from his old boss at the *New York Mirror*. Phil, a New Yorker, had worked on the *Mirror* before he married an Indianapolis woman and moved here. The *Mirror* wanted the story but Phil said he couldn't help them because he had already made a deal with the *Daily News*. But after some heavy cajoling and begging, Phil relented and wired the same story to the *Mirror*, a racy tabloid. When the *Daily News* learned of what he had done, the angry city editor called him back and told him the bonus had been cut to $125. The check from the *Mirror* was $50. Phil decided that a half a loaf was better than none.

Connie was the archetypal backstreet lover. Born Minnie Bell Conrad, she always went by the name Connie. Her father died when she was nine years old and her mother, who was caring for her four children, died two years later. Connie moved to Shelbyville, Kentucky, to live with an uncle, and then later moved in with other relatives, including an aunt, in Zionsville. She moved to Indianapolis and was graduated from Shortridge High School at the age of 20. Connie was smart, ambitious, a hard worker and known to have a sharp temper. In 1941 she was hired as a file clerk at Lilly. A year later she married Ray Kiefer but divorced him a few years later. In the mid-1950s she married Curtis Nicholas, although her passion continued to be reserved for Forrest Teel as it had been for a decade or more. Though she and Teel frequently traveled together, they were never together at the homes and the country club that Teel frequented. She was employed by then at Indianapolis Life Insurance Company.

At Lilly's, Teel's new interest, Laura Mowrer, was secretary to the head of sales training. She had been working at the company for five years. A co-worker described her as pleasant, personable, professional and very attractive. She kept her marriage secret while at Lilly's but got a divorce while living in Indianapolis.

When Laura picked up her copy of *The Star* the morning after the shooting and saw the headlines and Teel's photo, she was stunned. She raced to her office at Lilly's before other workers arrived, cleaned out her desk, grabbed up all of her personal items and left. She followed the advice of a savvy attorney, David Lewis, who told her she should tell the police what she knew and then get out of town. She told the police that Teel left his office about 5 p. m. and came directly to her apartment and left about 1 a. m.

Max Friedersdorf, who was reporting the story for *The News*, said he raced to the apartment early that morning after Laura had "flown the coop" but before the police arrived. He said he induced a maintenance man into letting him into her apartment.

"I rummaged around and found a nice photo of her which *The News* played up on the front page that day, scooping *The Star* and the *Times* big time," he said.

After being questioned by the police, Laura fled to California, escaping from a pack of frustrated reporters.

The police a few days later released some of the unsent letters that they found in Connie's apartment. Their contents kept the story on page one. One she had written to Teel contained her thoughts about the breakup. It read:

> I can now see that you were completely selfish in your love for me and because of this, many innocent people have been hurt.
>
> This has not been written in anger because I am still not angry with you, just hurt and heartbroken and my memories are of the wonderful hours that we did share and the few trips that we did take together. I am sorry that you failed me after all this time.
>
> I now know what I must do and it is something that I have given much thought to, because I have said before, life without

> you would have no meaning. My only fear is that I might fail —other than that I have absolutely none. Even though I know it is wrong, to me, it is much easier than seeing you and knowing that I can never again be as completely happy as I have been in the past.
>
> I still love you with all my heart and as you well know there is no half way point for me when I truly feel as I do about you.
>
> Connie

And in another undelivered letter to Teel dated July 22, nine days before shooting him, she wrote:

> I still love you and even though you are willing to come back I would never have that peace of mind and serenity that I have had for the past years in knowing that our love for one another was sincere.
>
> There might be another Laura and I just couldn't take it another time. It is most difficult for me to understand how you could turn to her so easily just because she was there and we had a misunderstanding.
>
> ...although you have offered me all that Betty [Mrs. Teel] has financially that is not what I want or have ever wanted unless I could have you as completely as I have for so many years.

She said in the letter that she had divorced her second husband, Curtis Nicholas, because she knew Teel didn't want to share her.

In a letter to Nicholas, who was living in Detroit, she wrote, "By the time you get this letter I plan to no longer be in this world." She apologized for the "anguish" caused him during their brief marriage.

In a letter to a friend, written on July 23, she told the woman to expect to find her body, and which relatives to notify and what to do with her possessions. She said she wanted to be cremated in her Chinese lounging robe and "blue ruffled gown" and her ashes scattered from an airplane over the runways of every airport in the Indianapolis area.

Teel's will was probated on August 6 three days after his death. He left his entire estate to his wife. The estate's estimated value was $150,000 and included their Washington Boulevard home, his new Cessna airplane and the Cadillac. His income was estimated at $80,000 a year—a major salary a half century ago. There was no mention of Connie or Laura in the will.

Connie spent the next eight months in General Hospital trying to recover from the paralysis in her arm and hand caused by the way she was lying in the car for eight hours. She was transferred to the Marion County Jail on March 13 to await her trial in a small courtroom in the basement of the dingy and rat-infested 81-year-old Marion County Courthouse. Covering the trial were reporters and photographers for the *Chicago Tribune*, *The New York Times*, and *Life* magazine. Other reporters came from Australia, Japan and England. An Indianapolis radio station broadcast the trial from the courtroom.

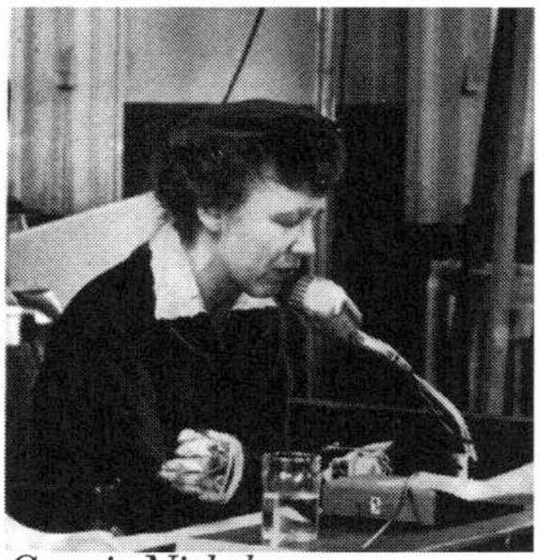

Connie Nicholas

Connie retained as her attorney Charles Symmes and he, in turn, selected his father, Frank Symmes, as co-counsel. Indianapolis attorney Joseph Quill later was added to the defense team. Chief deputy prosecutor Francis Thomason headed the prosecution. Attorney Judson Haggerty aided him.

The trial had been going on for three weeks before Connie took the stand, a risky decision for a defendant, but she felt certain that she could make a good impression on the jury.

"Connie was a real charmer," Friedersdorf said. "She was petite, gregarious, a nice smile and always available to talk to us."

On the day that she was to testify, Bob Early agreed that we should carry all of her testimony in the next day's paper. To do that we hired two court stenographers to work in shifts. One would record her testimony and leave the courtroom to type it at her office and then hand it to a copy boy, who brought it to the city desk. While the woman was typing, the second stenographer took over in the courtroom taking down Connie's answers to the lawyers' questions. The alternating shifts went on for several hours. Connie's testimony was as dramatic as expected, but she tended to be garrulous. She talked and gestured and talked. Oh how she talked throughout the afternoon and into the evening. The copy from the stenographers kept arriving. As soon as it was checked, it went to the composing room.

Deadlines came and passed. And still her testimony continued to arrive. It kept coming long after she had left the stand. By the time her last words had been sent to the composing room, it was 3 a.m. By then there had been several makeovers of the paper. Her testimony quickly filled the two open pages reserved for her testimony, but it began spreading into other pages, driving out other stories. By the time the last of her testimony was in the paper, Connie could brag that she had commandeered all of the news space in 17 pages, knocking out all of the women's pages, some wire stories and some local news. But, of course, no advertising.

Edward H. Frank, who covered the trial for us, recalled some of the public reaction to *The Star's* devoting that much space to Connie's testimony.

"I came in the office that Saturday to write a Sunday story on the trial, and Bob called me into his office," he recalled. "He said he had received many, many calls—some positive and some negative—about the voluminous Q and A in the paper. I remember asking him to ask the callers just one question. Did they read it? He said he already had and every caller said 'yes'."

The judge presiding was 35-year-old Thomas Faulconer, recently elected to the Criminal Court bench.

"In those days we competed against *The News* and the *Times*," Ed said. "I loved the competition. Tom Faulconer had been a friend of my sister I believe in high school. Anyway, it was late morning, about 11 a.m. when he called a brief recess just before Connie was to take the stand. I went back to his office and requested that he delay the start of the testimony until after lunch. He knew the reason, smiled, and agreed to do so. Of course, that made the afternoon papers furious."

After she took the stand Connie went into great detail about their backstreet affair. She said it began after she went to work at Lilly's in 1941 as a file clerk. She met Teel and after awhile he asked her out, but she rebuffed him for two years because Teel was a married man, she said. But after two years, she relented and they began seeing each other regularly, even after she was married to Kiefer and later to Nicholas. It went on for 15 years. She said he once paid off the balance on her car loan and on another occasion gave her $2,500, and that he faithfully paid her $100 monthly rent. And she told of Teel's promise to marry her. Details of their lives together were aired, including the last painful three weeks before their affair ended in his white Cadillac.

"There was another aspect to the trial that perhaps you will recall," Frank wrote me. "Late in the trial, perhaps the last few days. Early gave me an order that we no longer were to identify Forrest Teel as an Eli Lilly

The press awaiting the verdict in the Connie Nicholas trial.

executive, just as a business or drug company executive. I complained, saying that the Lilly name was being used by every other paper, including the wire services. Wouldn't we look foolish by not using the Lilly name? He said if I wanted to argue about it he would arrange an appointment for me to see 'the old man.' Of course, I didn't do such a thing and followed his orders. If you check the clips late in the trial, you will see that the Lilly name had been dropped."

The verdict came at 2:34 a.m. on April 15. The jury found her guilty of voluntary manslaughter, which carried a 2-to-21-year prison sentence. At first she threatened to appeal the verdict, complaining that her attorneys had done a poor job, but she thought better of it and left the day following the trial for the Indiana Women's Prison on the eastside of Indianapolis. When she was paroled after 22 months in prison, she took a new name and settled in the small town of New Whiteland just south of the city. That was the last we heard of her.

While all of this was going on, Betty Teel and her son moved into a smaller house in Crows Nest, another upscale northside neighborhood. By then she had become a chain smoker and an alcoholic, a combination that had tragic consequences. The house caught fire from one of her cigarettes on Jan. 2, 1960. She was rushed to the hospital with second and third-degree burns covering more than half of her body. She died four days later. It was the second fire at her home. Three months earlier her nightgown had caught fire from her cigarette, and she had spent two weeks in a hospital receiving skin grafts. Friends said their son Tommy never recovered from his dad's infamous life and death. After his mother died, he went to Texas to live with relatives. He died in his early 50s.

Laura stayed in California, at least until the trial was over, and while there were perfunctory attempts to locate her, we never really pursued her.

Friedersdorf wrote "the trial was a newspaperman's dream, i.e., sex, money, murder, Lilly's, a white Cadillac and mystery mistress."

Ed Frank spoke for most of us when he wrote, "Of all the stories I covered in the 11 years I spent at *The Star* that one would have to be at the top of the list."

It tops my list, too.

¤

15 • A Dingy Courthouse

Journalists staying in the city to cover the Connie Nicholas trial discovered that the real trial was being jammed into a courtroom in the basement of the dingy Marion County Courthouse. The ornate Second Empire architectural style building was 76 years old when I wrote a feature story about it in 1952. Here's what I wrote:

> The periodic cry to "tear down that eyesore of a courthouse" has risen again.
>
> Its wiring may be bad, as the State Fire Marshal recently declared, and it may be a rat and fire trap, as most people believe, but the ancient, musty Marion County Courthouse does have a distinctive personality.
>
> Unceremoniously celebrating its diamond anniversary this year, the county's governmental home daily sees a rare cross section of humanity roaming its corridors, offices and courtrooms.
>
> Take the homeless derelicts with unshaved faces and listless eyes who line the halls in the building's basement to escape the winter winds for a few hours each day.
>
> In the county clerk's office one floor above, a young couple hold hands beneath the counter. Confident, happy, they await their marriage license.
>
> Upstairs, hands apart, another couple—no longer so confident, so happy—sit stiffly in a judge's chamber and agree that a divorce is the only solution to their problems.
>
> Across the hall a young man weeps. A $14 holdup has just cost him 10 years of his life in the Indiana State Prison at Michigan City.
>
> In the coroner's office a frightened 15-year-old girl relates what she saw the night her father was murdered with a butcher knife.
>
> A woman sobs quietly in one of the small ante-rooms outside of the prosecutor's office.
>
> While happiness and tragedy lend poignancy, the building has its less dramatic facets.
>
> Courthouse workers chat cheerfully at the open lunch counter (run by Lou and Becky Faccone) on the main floor—unaware of the events taking place, which would make rich source

material for a novel. They have seen too much of it.

In the hallway, well-dressed attorneys converse with elderly politicians who still use armbands to hold up their sleeves. Frustrated citizens amble from room to room in search of their tax statements and a dusty workman waits for the elevator to take him to the third floor and the office of the building administrator.

Aside from the rich and varied human element, the Courthouse itself is a study in contrasts.

Of ancient design, its heavy walls and high ceilings carry ornate bas reliefs and beautiful paintings which are obscured in spots by thick layers of dirt.

Dark and ponderous looking, the structure often gives off such an oppressive form of steam heat that just being inside dries the mouth, induces yawns and tires the legs. Offensive smelling restrooms frequently have been the target of public criticism.

Beneath the Courthouse roof is an unoccupied section that even the rats find dry and uninviting. A seven-foot high tunnel runs from the basement to the County Jail—an underground route once used for transporting dangerous prisoners.

Many feel that the cost of the courthouse is in itself criminal. Completed in 1876 at an initial cost of $1,750,000, the building ultimately cost the taxpayers $4,258,174.07. Even before 1933 when the bonds and interest were finally written off, some citizens wanted the building torn down.

In a Sept. 11, 1927 edition of *The Indianapolis Star*, one reporter wrote: "There are many good citizens just itching to tear it down."

Today, officials are again investigating means of financing a new city-county skyscraper to replace the Courthouse. Those ideas are not new.

If past experience proves anything, the domeless gray structure probably will shrug off the current insults and make plans for celebrating its 100th anniversary in 1977.

But three years after the visiting journalists returned home, the Courthouse was gone. It was replaced on the same site in 1962 with a 28-story glass and steel structure to house the city and county government offices and courts. The building lacks the ambience of the ancient Courthouse. Scores of offices line the narrow hallways; a credit to the efficiency engineers who planned the building, but it might as well have signs on the doors saying "Keep Out."

Still it was an improvement over the bland State Office Building that opened in 1953 behind the Statehouse.

The City Hall, built in 1909, is still standing proudly at Ohio and Alabama streets, but its municipal government offices moved to the City-County Building when it was completed. The building is of neoclassical design with a central rotunda of 750 square feet topped with a stain-glass dome. The building stood idle for a dozen years and then became home for the State Museum, which had been housed in the basement of the Statehouse. The collection of stuffed birds and battle flags there hardly qualified it to be termed a museum, but a few quality items were added when it was moved to the City Hall.

When the new State Museum in White River State Park opened, the old City Hall was again without a tenant, but not for long. When work on the expansion and improvements to the Central Library got underway, the library moved all of its books and administrative offices into the building as a temporary home for its headquarters.

¤

16 • Our Monuments Disparaged

Years ago when sportswriters from the major newspapers spent a week or so at the Indianapolis Motor Speedway before the Memorial Day race and there wasn't enough activity—or preferably gore—at the track to fill a 20-inch column, they looked around for subjects in Indy-No-Place to pan. An accident at the track, hopefully one causing death or injury, made their day, allowing them to wring their journalistic hands.

But on those dull days when the track's best offer was a minor controversy among crew chiefs over some new regulation, the writers looked elsewhere for a column to justify billing the paper for a steak dinner at St. Elmo's.

It was always safe to lament the amount of carnage at the Speedway since the first 500-Mile Race in 1911, but that topic was worked over so often they turned their attention to mocking the city. A repeat target were the city's war memorials that tended to dominate an otherwise bland downtown in the 1960s.

Monument Circle

The Soldiers and Sailors monument on the Circle was generally selected for ridicule by one of those Mike Royko-wannabes, who noted its excessive adornments. The massive Indiana War Memorial came in for the razzing, too. Shaped like some huge Egyptian tomb, it really made a better target. The rusting military hardware on Obelisk Square across Michigan Street from the memorial was always worth a throwaway slur, and they managed to get in a jab about the adjoining American Legion headquarters.

It was a way to stir up a little controversy and make the citizens here fire off letters to the editor defending the city and castigating the "know-nothing" visiting scribes.

In fact, most Indianapolis residents were proud of the monuments, particularly the one on the Circle. And why not; it's the heart and center of the city. Both the monument and the site itself has an interesting history.

When Alexander Ralston, a gentle white-haired bachelor then in his fifties, laid out the city in 1821, he didn't envision the city growing any larger than the square mile he had selected. He divided the mile square into nine north-south streets and nine east-west streets, and his plan included four diagonal streets branching out. And he had the foresight to make the streets wide. In the center was a high, grassy knoll of nearly four acres, which he staked off into a circle with an 80-foot wide street running around it. It was to be the site of the governor's residence.

For a half dozen years, the site had been a pasture for horses, cows, sheep, goats and hogs, but in 1827 the area was fenced off and work began on a two-story brick residence for the governor and his family. The house was elaborate but impractical, lacking such necessities as a kitchen and pantry.

The governor, James Brown Ray, made it clear he didn't intend to live there and Mrs. Ray was horrified about having the townspeople watch her hang out her laundry in the center of town. As a result, the residence was left unfinished. Over the years, the building housed public offices, a bank, and later fell into disuse and became a haven for tramps, bats, rats and stray animals. It was sold at auction in 1857 and torn down. The grounds returned to pasture until well after the Civil War.

Veterans of that war lobbied for a monument for several years and in time the legislature and the Grand Army of the Republic put up the money to build one. President Benjamin Harrison laid the cornerstone at the site in 1888. It took a while but in 1902 the Soldiers and Sailors Monument was dedicated. Miss Liberty standing atop the monument's 284-foot shaft towered over the city. The ornate monument with its two fountains, and imposing statuary was a source of pride for the citizens then–and even now.

When the Commission for Downtown was formed during the Hudnut administration, its first major project was enhancing the site by replacing the asphalt on the Circle with red bricks in 1978.

The secondary target of the visiting sportswriters, the War Memorial, was built to honor the 130,000 Indiana men and women who served in World War I. The general assembly in 1920 authorized construction of a war memorial plaza that included a headquarters for the year-old American Legion. It took most of the 1920s to construct the mammoth War Memorial.

Criticism of the monuments has not deterred the city from honoring veterans of World War II, Korea and Vietnam with monuments to them in the War Memorial Plaza. And the nation's Congressional Medal of Honor winners are honored here with an unusual display overlooking the impressive canal that now runs through downtown Indianapolis. Located a few blocks north is still another monument, this one honoring the victims and survivors of the sinking of the USS Indianapolis at the end of World War II.

You defend the United States, you get honored in Indianapolis.

17 • A Photo Doctor

Lowell Parker was the paper's buffer between the staff and the volatile managing editor, Bob Early, while serving as city editor from 1949 until 1963 when he left to become managing editor of the *Phoenix Gazette*.

Parker was no micro-manager. He rarely edited copy, but he kept in close touch with the reporters. When an exciting story was in the works, Parker would rip off the edge of a sheet of copy paper and place it on his lip. If he got an outrageous order from Early, he didn't question him about it, he would simply drop it in the do-nothing drawer of his desk, figuring that it would die there. It usually did.

I like to picture Parker as a character in a Scott Fitzgerald novel. He was handsome, an excellent dancer. He loved to party and women loved him. He had seen much of the world (some of the travel thanks to airline press junkets), and he and his wife Hope had made frequent visits to Cuba before Fidel Castro took the fun and accessibility out of it. Parker had a fine sense of humor. When the wire services carried a story about the death of flamboyant actor Errol Flynn, Parker shook his head and said, "There aren't many of us left."

In the 1980s the matter of doctoring photographs was always good for an airing by earnest journalists and photographers in panel discussions on ethics at editors' conventions. The issue became a hotter topic after photographs could be altered digitally.

It was common practice for a staff artist to touch up a photo so it would print better. To conform to *The Star's* priggish standards, the artists were told to paint out the navels of young ladies wearing two-piece bathing suits (this before bikinis), or to minimize an arresting cleavage with a little airbrushing. But the artist did exceed the bounds of prudery one day when he turned a two-piece suit into a one-piece.

Parker wasn't bothered by ethical considerations when he issued an order one May to the photographers assigned to the Indianapolis Motor Speedway. The 500-Mile Race was always the city's premier event and almost daily throughout the month we'd carry a photo or two at the track. He knew that Early felt strongly about the Speedway, so he treated Speedway activities with care, though he personally had little regard for the race.

The order Parker issued to the photographers was to discourage radio announcer Sid Collins, the "Voice of the Speedway," from edging into photos of race drivers, car owners and whatever celebrity showed up at the track during the month.

Sid was an outstanding announcer and he was, indeed, the "Voice of the 500" on national radio for some 20 years, originating the phrase, "the greatest spectacle in racing." But Sid had an ego problem. He enjoyed seeing his name in print, hearing promos about himself on the radio, and seeing his picture in the newspapers. He managed to ingratiate himself with the celebrities who showed up at the track or at race-related social functions throughout the month.

Parker finally had enough of Sid showing up in the glossies coming out of the darkroom. At first he told the photographers to discourage Sid from pushing into the photo. If that didn't deter him, Parker told them to station him on the end so he could be cropped out of the picture.

The photographers didn't have much luck keeping Sid out of the pictures, but they did make sure he was easily cropable. After noticing that he had been excised from the last two pictures, Sid made sure the next time that he was safely in the middle of the group.

When the photo with a smiling Sid happily in the center showed up on Parker's desk one afternoon, Lowell grabbed a pair of scissors and cut the photo in half. He trimmed Sid from the photo, glued the two parts together and, with a grin on his face, sent it on to the engravers.

As a footnote, there was no complaint from either Sid or the photo staff about what was clearly a violation of journalistic ethics. But those kinds of infractions didn't get much attention from the journalistic overseers in those years.

One photo that was doctored did produce a flood of comments from both the public and the Speedway. Again the culprit was a photo hog, who showed up once too often on the edges of a crash scene at the track. Photographer Frank Fisse said that Early had ordered him to keep the man out of any future pictures. But sure enough the guy showed up in a shot of another crash site. Other than the photo hog in it, the photo was worth running in the paper, so Frank—to avoid incurring Early's wrath—said he asked artist Gil Sweeney to change the guy's face. Instead, Gil airbrushed him completely out of the picture and replaced him with a tree. The tree looked so authentic that the Speedway began getting calls from readers complaining that it was dangerous having a tree there. We heard from the Speedway about it and Frank said he checked with the Star's switchboard operators. They told him that they had received at least 35 calls about the dangerous tree at the track.

¤

18 • Our Hatchet Man

I worked with Lester Hunt for 13 years, but I don't believe I ever really knew him. Before I was named an assistant city editor in 1953 I had worked at a desk next to Lester's for two years. He was friendly and helpful but he was never one of the boys. Few, if any, of the reporters and editors were close to him. Lester was older than most of us. He was 51 when he joined the paper in 1948—a year before I was hired.

Lester Hunt often riled the readers.

He seemed to operate apart from the rest of the staff. He got many of his assignments from the publisher, either directly or through Bob Early. To politicians, mostly Democrats but some Republicans, too, Les Hunt was *The Star's* "hatchet man." When Pulliam decided that some politician or bureaucrat got out of line, it was Lester's task to bring him back in line or put him down. He managed it skillfully.

He had many sources that he could call on to feed him facts and rumors and innuendos to skewer the target of the moment. He worked the phones quietly and ceaselessly. He was a master at squeezing information out of people. Most of his stories were played on page one. They did not always pass the scrutiny that editors gave other local stories proposed for the front page.

As a reporter and writer he was always professional. His copy was clean and needed very little editing. He bragged that he was educated in the public schools of New York City. He educated me one afternoon when I responded to a caller on the phone, "This is him." "No, no," he said, "This is he."

There were many times when I appreciated having Les Hunt in the city room when a difficult assignment came across the desk. He was fearless in dealing with legislators and office holders, though I never heard him raise his voice. He got things accomplished with little fuss. And, surprisingly, Lester got along well with many of the politicians he skewered. Many an evening Andrew Jacobs Sr. would drop by to have dinner with Lester. Jacobs, a Democrat, had served one term in Congress, and he managed to make Pulliam's blacklist over some criticism of the Pulliam paper's treatment of President Truman. Jacobs, in fact, was Lester's lawyer. They made a curious twosome; the dapper Hunt walking down the hall with the tall, Lincolnesque Jacobs in his rumpled black suit.

Lester always wore a suit and rarely doffed his jacket. He wore white-on-white shirts with cufflinks. He had his idiosyncrasies. He told me one day that he fertilized his garden with his own urine, bottling it at home. And he liked to say that he didn't wash his hands after urinating. He did it before.

He came to *The Star* with a fascinating background—and I never heard how or why he was hired.

He was the son of a banker and promoter. By the age of 15 he had lived in 24 states. He served with the Army's 27th Division on the Mexican border and later during World War I. He began his newspaper career in New York at the age of 20, but he spent 20 years on the West Coast. Even then he riled public officials. While writing about the Ku Klux Klan in Tacoma, Washington, in the 1920s, he was kidnapped and taken to a Klan initiation ceremony. The next day he wrote a story critical of the ceremony. In 1939 he refused to tell a judge where he was getting information about a grand jury investigation of bribery and was sentenced to 10 days in jail. Then he wrote about life in jail.

He was hired by the Teamsters Union as a troubleshooter and publicity man. In 1941 he moved to the Teamsters headquarters in Indianapolis to edit the union's magazine. He became a knowledgeable adviser to union officials, but when Dave Beck became head of the union he fired Lester. That was in 1948. A year later Lester joined *The Star*. I never learned who hired him, though I assumed it was Pulliam.

He was often at the Statehouse on political and legislative assignments. Aware that press conferences often were called to gain the subject some attention in the press, Lester tended to dismiss them as marginal producers of news. And when television crews began showing up with their cumbersome cameras, wiring and klieg lights, Lester viewed them as nuisances. Teaming with Eugene Jepsom Cadou, head of UPI's Indiana bureau, they would wait until the cameras began to roll and then interrupt the speaker by asking an embarrassing question or enlivening it with an obscenity.

To accommodate the TV crews, the legislative chambers were hung with large ball-like lights that were so bright that some reporters were forced to wear sunglasses. Not Cadou. A tall, imposing figure, Jep marched up to the podium one afternoon, grabbed the microphone and bellowed, "Is there no relief from these electronic bastards?"

Jep's most memorable remark was a description of Hoosier Hysteria as "a bunch of pimply-faced kids running around in their underwear."

He was unfazed by rank. At a press conference called by Governor George N. Craig, Jep took umbrage after the governor had evaded answering five questions. He stood up, announced, "These proceedings are unworthy of my attention," and walked out.

Both Jep and Lester were the type of newsmen who pitched in to do routine reporting and writing when their staffs were stretched thin.

Lester enhanced his reputation when he tackled secrecy in the state welfare department in the 1950s, and exposed election fraud in Lake County in 1960 and 1961.

He was also instrumental in helping to expose the state highway scandals during the Craig administration (1953-57).

He worked at the paper until 1962 when he died at the age of 67. Each year since his death the paper has given the Lester M. Hunt Award to a reporter deemed to have done the best investigative work for the year.

¤

18 • We Got Scooped

Lester Hunt may have helped expose corruption in the state's highway department, but it was Phil Clifford—with some pushing from the managing editor—who did most of the groundwork.

The dapper Clifford joined the paper in 1955 after having worked on papers in several states. In 1949 he won a Pall Mall Award while working for the *New York Daily Mirror* by helping to capture a fugitive murderer. In a time when reporters sometimes made news themselves, Phil later served as the murderer's best man when he got married just before he was executed. The highway investigation began after Bob Early was tipped off that state highway employees had been claiming per diem expenses for inspecting highway right-of-way while they were stumping for Governor George Craig. Per diem cheating, it developed, was just one sin of many in the department. Several reporters assigned to check the reports came up empty, but Early was convinced that his source was sound, so he called Clifford into his office and told him to keep digging full time.

Phil Clifford was an Edward R. Murrow look-a-like.

Phil reported periodically that it was slow going, but after two months of poring over reports and highway contracts, his digging began to pay off. It was more than a few lower-level bureaucrats cheating on their expense vouchers. The probe shifted to examining executives in the department and land buyers. Lester was assigned to help Phil deal with targets of the probe and to ask some of the tough questions.

The plan was to break a series of stories on Sunday, April 14, 1957, but when John V. Wilson, the Statehouse reporter for the *Indianapolis Times*, learned what we planned, the *Times* decided to break the story on the prior Thursday.

Wilson recalled that the scandals occurred while Craig was governor but the story broke early in the succeeding administration of Governor Harold Handley. "That whole Handley administration could be described as anti-Craig," Wilson said.

"A highly placed highway official (as they say) and another elected state official suggested (not very specifically) that I look through purchasing records," Wilson informed me a half century later. "I spent several days in the Statehouse basement and came up with a few things that I discussed with Leibo [Irving Leibowitz, *Times* managing editor]. Leibo also checked some of them with his sources at the Statehouse. We were a day or two away from putting it all on paper when Leibo got word that *The Star* was working on it, so he rushed to print."

R. K. Shull, then a city desk reporter on the *Times*, credited Leibo with staging the journalistic coup. He said he made up the front page of the early edition with startling headlines and stories but few specifics about the scandal.

"That first edition looked good but it didn't have hardly a single fact in it, but by the afternoon several of us managed to come up with enough stories to take the edge off of whatever *The Star* was planning," Shull recalled.

At *The Star* we had to acknowledge—but bitterly—the *Times's* coup. It forced us to break the series the next day. We also felt that it robbed Clifford of a chance for a Pulitzer Prize.

The highway scandal was a familiar one. Persons with inside information bought property in the way of planned road development and sold it to the state at inflated prices. There was bribery involved, false claims, phony notarizations, and some of the same land was sold two and three times.

Criminal charges were brought against 12 persons, including high state officials. In a trial in the basement of the old Courthouse in 1958, a jury convicted three major figures—Virgil (Red) Smith, the chairman of the Indiana Highway Commission, William Sayer, Governor Craig's administrative assistant (sometimes referred to as "assistant governor"), and Elmer (Little Doc) Sherwood, a wily politician and public relations practitioner.

Sherwood had such clout that he spent hours in Craig's office when the Governor was out politicking. With Sayer's acquiescence, Sherwood would plop himself in Craig's chair, plant his feet on the desk and work the phones, setting up deals with highway contractors eager to do business with the state; always letting the person know where the call was coming from.

Jep Cadou Sr. once asked Governor Craig at the Indianapolis Press Club, "If something should happen to Sherwood, would you become governor?"

Leroy New, who served as chief trial deputy for the Marion County

Prosecutor, said a few weeks before he died in 2005 that though he was a close friend of Sayer, it didn't deter him from leading the prosecution against him.

He said the trio split the millions in kickbacks equally, and all three went to the Indiana State Prison at Michigan City.

And not, incidentally, any hopes Craig may have had for further advancement in politics was ended.

Phil Clifford's life was a series of peaks and valleys. During World War II, he served in the Office of Strategic Services (OSS), precursor of the CIA, but Phil never discussed his duties in the organization. In his early years as a reporter, he had a serious drinking problem. That appeared to have ended when he married an Indianapolis woman, who induced him to settle in Beech Grove in a tidy little bungalow. A strong-willed woman, she stabilized his life. They were middle-aged when they married and had no children.

When I told him I was getting married in the fall of 1956, Phil said he couldn't understand why anyone would want to get married and start a family with the world in disarray. The current evidence of disarray was Egypt's Premier Gamel Abdel Nasser nationalizing the Suez Canal, causing Israel to invade Egypt and British and French forces to seize the canal. But as the sage said, "This too shall pass."

Phil was baffled by the persistent grief shown by the parents who lost one of their eight children. "I can't understand it," he told me. "They still have seven other kids."

Despite his somewhat flamboyant background, Phil was not the sort of reporter who relished facing hostile targets. He was happy to take early retirement. He would occasionally visit friends in the city room. But after his wife died, Phil again turned to alcohol, and he died a few years later.

¤

20 • A Revered Columnist

If Lester Hunt riled the readers, Tom Keating placated them.

For 14 years Tom's column was the most widely read feature in the paper. Somehow each day—five days a week—he managed to find a story about an interesting person, place or thing that he passed along to readers in clear, simple prose, usually in 700 words. Thousands of readers turned to his column each morning.

Writing three columns a week is the norm for most columnists. Writing five can be daunting, but Tom brushed aside any suggestion that he cut back to three a week. He didn't like to give up that space in the paper. And he rarely turned out a clunker.

He wrote about ordinary people doing some extraordinary things. It might be about a grocer or a politician, a cop, coach or a housewife. It was his belief that everyone has done something in his or her past that was memorable enough to make a column. If it interested Tom, he believed it would interest his readers. And he was right. He wrote the column—roughly 3,300 of them—from 1971 to 1985.

Tom Keating

I doubt that he would get a second look today if he applied for a job at the paper where applicants must bring an impressive resume just to qualify for the next step, a series of examinations. When he walked into the city room that Saturday morning in the fall of 1966 to apply for a reporting job (his third attempt, I learned only recently) he had been selling real estate and managing an apartment building. He attended Ball State University for a year before dropping out. That background was hardly the credentials for a job on the state's biggest newspaper. He was 26, married with two children.

Sometimes in those years we hired beginning reporters without a lot of background checking. If they looked and acted promising, and there was an opening, there was a good chance they'd be hired. But with Tom, it was more than that. He struck me as intelligent and self-assured, knowledgeable about the city, and obviously eager to work on a newspaper. I knew his father slightly and I knew the neighborhood where he grew up because I grew up there, too, though some 15 years earlier.

A sports addict, Tom had hoped to make the Ball State football team as a walk-on but it didn't work out. A bum knee, as I remember him telling me. He came back to Indianapolis and married 20-year-old Gloria O'Connor when he was 22. After his athletic career ended, he spent years coaching boys in Catholic Youth Organization programs and at Tabernacle Presbyterian Church.

Taking a job that paid very little to first-year reporters was a risk, but he was happy to take it. I believe it was the best hire I made in 41 years at *The Star*.

After a couple of weeks of writing obits and short items, we sent him to the police beat, as we did with most new reporters. He quickly shined there, coming up with stories that other reporters had missed. He didn't always follow the standard routine of dutifully checking each police report, though he missed very little. If he put checking the reports on hold, it was because he was chasing a story in some other part of the City-County Building.

After a few months on the police beat, he became a general assignment reporter. Even then he had an uncanny ability to come up with feature stories, or enhance an otherwise routine assignment into a page one story by capturing some element that most of us would have overlooked.

One Saturday morning I sent him and photographer Frank Fisse to cover a talk by Ralph Abernathy, head of the Southern Christian Leadership Conference, at a church. When they returned to the city room, Tom came in with two feature stories that he had picked up along the way, as well as a story about Abernathy. Where most reporters would have written a few paragraphs about Abernathy's remarks, Tom portrayed the service as an old-fashioned revival, demonstrating Abernathy's deftly bringing out "amens" and "yeah brothers" and harmonious hand clapping and foot stamping. He put readers into the church that day.

When the daily columnist, Lowell Nussbaum, decided to retire in 1971 after 26 years writing "The Things I Hear," a collection of brief items about people and doings in the city five days a week, we took a gamble and replaced him with Keating. Tom didn't rely on short items phoned in by readers, he wrote each column as a complete feature story.

Lowell Nussbaum was a tall, strong but gentle person with a background of reporting and desk work on the *Indianapolis Times* before bringing his column to *The Star*. Readers felt comfortable with his column. Lowell had been a leading promoter of a zoo for the city. After the zoo had finally opened Lowell escorted a delegation around the grounds. When they got to the tiger cage, he reached through the bars to pet one of his favorite tigers. That time, the usually placid tiger grabbed his arm and bit a large hunk out of it. Lowell never blamed the tiger, of course, but his arm was never the same.

Local columns usually are among the best read features in the paper. Lowell's daily collection of brief items was no exception. But his replacement soon had phenomenal success in bringing in readers. He made no overt moral judgments and he was careful to keep his opinions out of the column, but the choice of subjects reflected his views on life. It might be a homeless man trying to visit churches on Thanksgiving only to find the church doors locked. Or watching a young couple sadly refusing to look at each other as a judge questions them during a divorce hearing.

He wrote about neighbors ransacking a house, believing its residents had left and weren't coming back. They stripped the house of furniture, appliances, televisions and whatever looked worthwhile in a single day only to see the owners pull up in their driveway the next day.

Some of his columns read like short stories. I surmised that Tom embellished his stories with a few dramatic touches, but no matter. He had a sense of the comic and offbeat. Readers, especially women, loved him and his columns because he was never afraid to show a little tenderness. Often he had to leave his cramped office to get away from the telephone.

His wife, Gloria, remembers driving her children somewhere while Tom was in the back seat writing his column on a scratch pad. When he finished it, he told Gloria to stop at a phone booth so he could dictate his column to a secretary at the paper.

Tom wrote his column at national political conventions and he traveled to Israel and Moscow and found human interest stories wherever he went.

He was a voracious reader—history, literature, biographies, sports, and theology. Often he'd be deep in a book at three in the morning. It was part of his self-education, though he would never admit it.

"Tom was very intelligent and he had a high IQ," Gloria said, "but at Cathedral High School he was a little bored…he had a few problems with the brothers." In those days Tom and his cronies could be a bit unruly.

"He was a good person all around, a wonderful father and husband," she said. "I never saw a mean side to him."

But I did one night when I looked out the window of the newsroom and saw Tom and Harley Bierce, a reporter, slugging each other on the sidewalk on New York Street. It followed an argument in one of the grungy taverns near the paper. They were friends again the next day.

Gloria said that he was something of a loner, "but I was, too." She believed it was the result of his being an only child. She was an only child for nine years, too, she said. Tom often slipped away unnoticed to attend the noon Mass at St. Mary's Catholic Church a few blocks from the paper.

Keating never forgot his roots and would dismiss anyone who was full of himself, but he didn't lack confidence in his own abilities. I never had any success in passing him a tip on a story. If he accepted a suggestion, I think he felt it was no longer his idea, so I stopped trying. He didn't need my tips, anyway. He won a score of journalism awards.

When he compiled several of his better columns in a self-published book that he titled, *Indiana Faces and Other Places*, I suggested that he ask a copy editor to read it. He didn't see any reason to ask for help. The book, a collection of his columns, was rife with grammatical and spelling errors; once again demonstrating that a writer can't spot his own mistakes. I guess he figured he didn't need any assistance because he had been teaching a writing class at IUPUI. The book was published in 1982 and it sold well, anyway.

After 14 years writing the column, he decided to leave the paper in 1985 to take a job at Lilly Endowment. I think the diabetes that had troubled him for several years had gotten worse. He was tired.

Before he left, he said, "I've enjoyed the hell out of this, but you feel after a while you could write the history of the world in 700 words."

Seven months after leaving *The Star* he died in bed. His wife and their daughter, Kerrie, and her mother were in Chicago at the time.

"I called home that morning because Tom hadn't been feeling well," Gloria said. "I asked Kiernan how his dad was feeling, and he said he was still asleep. I told him to go check on him. He came back to tell me he was dead."

Kiernan, the youngest of their four children, was 14. "It was awful for him," she said.

The year after Tom died at the age of 45, the Indianapolis Press Club, with financial help from Lilly Endowment Inc. and the Indianapolis Foundation, started an annual feature writing competition among Indiana college students. The Thomas R. Keating Feature Writing Contest is conducted each year on a November weekend. Michael J. Quinn, an ex-Star reporter and friend of Tom's, has organized the contest each year with help from current and former Star staff members.

Discovering and encouraging potential Tom Keatings has been one of the goals of the contest.

21 • The Metaphor Maker

Sportswriters turn out some of journalism's more colorful writing. Perhaps it's the freedom—or license—they've been given to transform a routine ball game into an event of passing importance. A few of the practitioners hit the mark with their metaphors and similes, but too many make us wince when they reach for a comparison that fails to connect.

Bob Collins was one of the few who made the connections with grace, wit and style

He spent 43 years in *The Star's* playground, the last 27 as sports editor. While a student at Butler University, he joined the paper in 1948 as a temporary reporter, planning to stay three weeks. He never left.

Collins at his best: "Ben Hogan, living in the autumn of a fabled golfing career, reached back yesterday and found another springtime."

Like many newspapermen of his time, Bob was a romantic. It wasn't the dream of turning out the great American novel that nagged him. His dream was more modest. He felt that he had been born 20 years too late; that he belonged with the expatriates living in Paris in the Twenties. Bob would have enjoyed being a member of the Lost Generation, sipping cognac with Fitzgerald and Hemingway, and discussing novels in progress—a not uncommon dream of newspapermen a half century ago.

Bob fantasized about a lot of things. As the years muddled his memory, he had convinced himself that he had been an outstanding athlete—"pound for pound the best halfback in Cathedral High School's history;" an assessment he attributed to some unnamed coach. In truth, he was a third-stringer.

Much of his fantasizing could be traced to his fondness—nay his passion—for spirits, manhattans being the favored drink. Alcohol dogged him for most of his life. Bob had an overriding talent that made coworkers overlook some of his frequent absences from the office. He was an outstanding writer and he knew it, but he liked to have the concurrence of others. A couple of years after he had retired and was already into extra innings, he would ask, "I was the best, wasn't I?" and I assured him he was. I had worked at the paper for almost as long as Bob, most of it on the news side, but Bob's stories and columns were one of the first things I turned to each morning before reviewing the day's output. His prose was one of the paper's bonuses.

To Collins, though, it wasn't enough that he had won more than 40 awards, he needed to go out with some hope that his reputation was secure. When his turn for induction into the Indiana Journalism Hall of Fame was announced, Bob began coercing dozens of friends and co-workers to attend the induction ceremony at the hall's home at DePauw University. Other inductees usually were satisfied with a cheering section of a wife and kids, and a co-worker or two.

"I don't know why I'm here," one of the Collins cadre remarked on that spring morning in 1990, "but Collins said I had to be here."

In the autumn of his career, Collins had lost his desire to cover sports events, unless it was a major golf tourney or a heavyweight championship boxing match. He had seen it all, he felt, so many of his columns were little more than earlier pieces reworked to tie in with a current event. But even his retreads sparkled with wit and feeling.

Bob Knight, the former Indiana University basketball coach, in a guest column for Collins wrote: "I invited him to a game in 1981 and said that we'd go out to eat afterward. At the half, I got a note from him telling me that he was going on to the restaurant as the game hadn't changed much since the last one he'd seen in 1958."

I wouldn't say that he was the paper's best reporter, though he did get his share of scoops, but I thought he was its best writer.

Few sportswriters could top him as a writer of lively prose. Journalism has little room for the poet but Collins occasionally qualified as one. The key to his success was his ability to lace his copy with colorful metaphors and similes. Even Aristotle recognized their value, telling us 2300 years ago that "the greatest thing by far is to be a master of metaphor. It is the one thing that cannot be learned from others, and it is a sign of genius."

I don't know that I would tag Collins as a genius, but he certainly helped us appreciate the beauty of a choice metaphor and its poor relation, the simile. Collins said he couldn't account for his gift.

"They just come to me," he said. "I don't try to dream them up."

Nor was he one of those less gifted writers who borrow other writer's metaphors, but the number and broad range of books he devoured heightened his imagination and gave him an appreciation of memorable writing.

Over the years Collins covered most of the major athletic events in the

United States and many abroad, including the Olympics. His favorite was the annual Masters golf tournament held each April in Augusta, Georgia.

He was there in 1967 when Ben Hogan teed off. Hogan's golfing career should have ended 16 years earlier when he suffered critical injuries in an automobile crash, but he was still competing at the age of 53. Bob began his column about the little iceman with these lines:

> Ben Hogan, living in the autumn of a fabled golfing career, reached back yesterday and found another springtime. And for one day, at least, it was his golf tournament—his crowd, his world, again. You could feel the emotion. It swept the Augusta National golf course like a sudden rainstorm as the little man who has been called the greatest golfer of all time marched over the sun-kissed fairways with those peculiar stiff-legged strides.
>
> It was like watching your past race in front of your eyes. And every man here yesterday enjoyed keeping an unexpected rendezvous with another era. It was like bumping into your high school sweetheart and discovering that she hadn't changed; like returning to the old swimming hole and finding the dead sycamore tree still leaning out over the water.

It's unlikely that Collins, a city boy, ever saw a swimming hole and wouldn't know a sycamore from a cherry tree. But no matter.

Bob was back at the Masters in 1983 to tell us about another aging legend, this one Arnold Palmer. He began:

> Leaks in the sky were patched just before noon. The sun smiled through—and there he was, stalking Augusta National again.
>
> The years rolled away and for a brief, shining moment it was Camelot. The old king—gray on top and wearing an extra set of eyes, but still stoking the competitive fires—hit charge on the bugle.
>
> And the army came limping and hopping, ready to throw every last ounce of the diminishing stamina into a final battle. Like their hero, members of Arnie's Army are getting a bit long in the tooth. They sort of stumble into step and take the hills

> carefully. Many appear to have bivouacked over a few too many meals. As a military group it looked more like the last encampment of the Grand Army of the Republic.

A bit overstated perhaps but it was sports copy—and overstatement in sports copy is tolerated.

Bob learned from trial and error how to keep the business office at bay with his skillful expense accounts. But not always.

He had been on the West Coast covering the Super Bowl, so the story goes, when he and some of his California wordsmith friends decided to visit Las Vegas before winding up the week. It was an unwise decision. It forced Collins to wire the managing editor, Bob Early, with this message: "Old money gone. Send new."

Early sent the money rather than have his sports editor marooned in Sin City, but when Collins returned, Early ordered him into his office to give an accounting of why he needed the extra cash. Collins confessed that he had lost his expense money at the gaming tables.

The managing editor, whose outbursts were legendary, supposedly told Collins, "Well since you didn't lie about it, we'll take care of it."

But the expense account didn't satisfy the business office and so the voucher came back to Early. After the third rejection, Early submitted a new one, accounting for the expense as "research on a future story." That one went through.

Bob was asked to speak at various events over the years. He was as witty with a microphone as he was with a typewriter, and audiences liked his talks. But the audience didn't respond one night in Columbus, Indiana. He told me that he used all of his best lines but he simply couldn't connect. There was only a smattering of laughs. He said he was so disturbed that he asked Stu Huffman, the editor of the *Columbus Republic*, why he had bombed.

Collins said Stu told him, "You didn't bomb, Bob...J. Irwin Miller was in the audience, and when J. Irwin laughs, everybody laughs," he said. "But when J. Irwin doesn't laugh, nobody laughs."

Miller was the city's premier industrialist, financier and philanthropist; the man credited with being responsible for underwriting most of the outstanding architecture that has made Columbus a tourist attraction. But J. Irwin was not known for his levity.

In addition to his daily "Sports Over Lightly" column, Bob also wrote a back page humor column twice a week. He called it "The Lighter Side."

In one of his Lighter Side columns at a time before militant feminists turned the American male into a minority, Bob was commenting on two unusual car crashes attributed to females that week. He wrote:

> A chink here, a chink there, the world slowly is being destroyed by women drivers.
>
> Many a back fence has gone to its place in the woodpile because a woman became momentarily confused and thought the "R" on the shift lever stood for rest. And many is the guy who has ended up taking the grass track down the street for foolishly assuming a gal drying her fingernails out the window was signaling a turn.

Collins often sprinkled his column with the antics of one or more of his six children. Married three times, Bob admitted he blew his first marriage after three decades, confessed that the second marriage never got started, but in his twilight years he met Kristen. He was 58. She was 36, a widow with two teenage daughters, and working at a downtown bar.

After they married, they opened a restaurant on the south side of Indianapolis. Bob's craving for recognition was realized there. Bobby Joe's Beef & Brew Restaurant is still thriving. Its walls are still lined with photos of Robert J. with friends and the famous.

The marriage seemed to work, especially for Collins, who was ailing in those last years. Kristen found herself taking care of him. She rushed him to hospital emergency wards a half dozen times before he died in 1995 at the age of 68.

¤

22 • Copy Boys Come and Go

We had a regular turnover in copy boys. Most of them were high school students but a few were attending college or art school. This was in the years before they were called copy messengers, reflecting the admission of girls to the ranks.

The jobs weren't demanding—carrying copy and galley proofs to various desks, filling paste pots, running errands, getting coffee for staff members. A few of the young men moved up and became reporters and photographers. In later years we raised the standards and gave aspirants provisional status as reporters so long as they were studying for a college degree. Drop out of college and it was back to fetching coffee.

The News didn't have the turnover in copy boys like we did at *The Star*. Two of theirs had been with the paper for many years. Both were a bit slow mentally but they carried out their duties in a satisfactory manner. The staff was protective of them.

One of them loaded down with papers just off the presses reportedly asked a man in the elevator he was sharing, "Press 2, will you bub?" The man—Gene Pulliam—dutifully pressed 2.

Ed Ziegner, *The News's* political writer, said he was standing in line at the bank waiting to cash his paycheck when one of the pair looked over his shoulder and noticed that the amount on Ed's check was larger than his. "Oh, that's right," he said. "You type."

We had a few learning impaired copy boys, too. One was told to drive the staff car to Richmond on the eastern edge of the state to pick up a photograph to illustrate a story.

"How do I get there?" he asked. The harried desk editor gruffly told him, "Just get on Washington Street (U. S. 40) and go and call us when you get to Richmond. We'll tell you where to go when you get there. It should take you about an hour. Get going."

An hour later the copy boy called to say he couldn't find Richmond.

"Where are you?" the editor asked.

"I'm in Terre Haute."

He'd gotten on Washington Street all right but he'd turned right instead of left.

¤

23 • A Tragic Night

I would rate our coverage of the explosion at the Fairgrounds Coliseum in 1963 as the paper's best coverage of spot news in all of the years that I spent at *The Star.*

The explosion happened on a rainy Halloween night on the opening night of the Holiday on Ice's 11-day run. It had been a fun-filled evening for the 4,300 spectators as some 36 of the 65 members of the company launched into the closing Mardi Gras number.

Just then a massive explosion in the south stands hurled a 50-foot section of the box seats, chairs, huge hunks of concrete, and spectators high in the air and on to the ice. A tower of flame shot to the ceiling. The blast erupted at 11:04 p. m.—two hours and 26 minutes before the paper's final edition was set to roll off of the presses.

It became the worst tragedy in the city's history. The blast killed 74 persons, wounded more than 400, and devastated hundreds of survivors both at the Coliseum and in homes across the state.

I had just fallen asleep at home a mile and a half north of the Coliseum when the phone rang. It was Bob Early barking, "Get to the Coliseum. There's been an explosion." When I sleepily asked what it was all about, he shouted, "Just get down there." I sat on the edge of the bed trying to decide if my socks matched when my wife, Patty, said, "Quit worrying about your socks. Just get dressed and get going."

And I did, racing to the Fairgrounds while sirens blared all across the northside. Soon every policeman and fireman available raced to the scene, as well as a stream of ambulances. I knew that it must be serious.

As I walked in, a tiny elderly woman, blood running down her face, was moaning, "Help me!" Then she wandered outside. I walked inside and couldn't believe what I was seeing. Dazed and injured people were wandering around. Out on the ice I saw bodies lying there. I didn't realize they were dead until I had walked in and around some of them. There on the ice were huge hunks of cement some three and four feet thick. I looked in the stands where the blast had erupted and could hardly believe what I was seeing. Where the stands had been was a huge cavity.

Within minutes more than a dozen *Star* reporters and photographers showed up. The scene shocked all of them, too. But we didn't have time to talk about what we were seeing. As the new city editor, it was up to me to assign the reporters to cover aspects of the tragedy, despite how they felt about seeing the victims. The photographers already were capturing

65 KILLED, HUNDREDS HURT IN COLISEUM GAS EXPLOSION

The Coliseum explosion aftermath as displayed on page one of The Star. *That's Connor on far right talking to reporter George Clements.*

the carnage. Soon we had reporters gathering the names of the victims, interviewing survivors, and talking to police and firemen. I assigned one reporter to find out what had caused the explosion.

Soon after the coroner, Dennis Nicholas, arrived, he ordered a makeshift morgue set up on the ice. Firemen and policemen placed bodies on sheets of plywood in rows on the ice. A command post was set up across the street where families waited for information. They were brought in to identify the dead and injured.

Many of the injured were taken into the adjoining Cattle Barn where they were placed in ambulances, buses and taxis and rushed to the city's hospitals.

Back in the newsroom calls went out to reporters at their homes to drive to the city's hospitals to gather information as the injured were brought in. By press time about 40 newsroom employees were working on the story.

I had ordered a copy boy to stand by one of the phones in the Coliseum lobby and to keep the line open to the city room and absolutely not allow anyone to get at it. At midnight I sent one of the photographers to gather the film from the other photographers and get back to the photo lab so that we'd be able to have pictures in the paper.

The cause of the blast was traced to a propane tank used to warm pre-popped popcorn. It was leaking from a faulty valve in the concession area beneath the stands. The vapors leaked into an unventilated room beneath the stands. When fumes reached an electric heater in the room, the massive explosion followed.

Dick Roberts was one of the reporters sent to the Coliseum. He was wandering around taking it all in. He was obviously upset and was not the sort of reporter I'd assign to get a body count. I told him to go back to the office and write a story about his impressions. He did and composed a page-one story that captured the scene. It read:

> You walked into a nightmare.
>
> This was the worst thing I have seen since combat in World War II.
>
> The lights above still cast the bluish light they cast onto the Ice Show.
>
> A red satin slipper lay on the ice.
>
> Three feet away was a pool of blood.
>
> The ice was white. In a second, you noticed more pools of blood, some still flowing.
>
> Ambulances screamed in and out of the Fairgrounds entrance. Never have so many emergency vehicles gathered at one place in Indiana.
>
> Bodies littered the ice.
>
> A handsome young man cradled the face of a beautiful young woman with enamel-white skin. She was a survivor. Specks of blood marred the whiteness of her skin.

> A gray-haired man lay on his back staring lifelessly at the ceiling.
> Ambulance attendants threw a gray blanket across him.
> A gray-haired woman in a brown dress lay on her side in a V-position. She wore a golden bracelet with red stones that still sparkled under the floodlights, but her hand was the gray of death.
> A blanket shrouded the face and form of a young woman in black pumps and a party dress. Only her ankles and thin wrists protruded...
> No one was crying.
> The shock was too strong for tears....
> Scattered between the bodies were chunks of reinforced concrete as big as three and four feet in size and weighing up to several hundred pounds.
> The city outside, between downtown and the fairgrounds, howled with sirens and streamed with blinking, spinning red lights on ambulances and police cars constantly after the blast.
> The fairgrounds itself was almost like a battleground, the surrounding streets thick with police and the edges of the streets jammed with crowds like war refugees, slowing the movement of ambulances and fire engines.

In addition to Roberts's vivid impressions, we put together a comprehensive account of the tragedy, complete with pictures, a listing of the dead and partial listing of the injured, and a separate about the cause of the blast.

The coverage earned the paper several journalism prizes, including the coveted National Headliners Award, which is selected by a panel of working journalists.

Later the Marion County Grand Jury investigated the causes of the explosions. The jury brought in seven indictments against state and city fire officials, Coliseum representatives and the firm that furnished the bottled gas. But none of the indictments resulted in convictions. It was four years after the tragedy that an out-of-court settlement of all of the claims growing out of the explosion was announced. It amounted to $3,555,000.

¤

24 • A Wave of Tornadoes

We all felt good about the way we covered the Coliseum disaster, but we didn't do much back patting over our coverage of the Palm Sunday tornadoes that battered Indiana two years later.

Even though tornadoes are common in the Midwest, reporting about them is difficult. It's not unusual for it to take hours and even days before authorities can come up with any definitive report on the number of persons killed or injured, and the amount of damage inflicted by a single tornado.

And when waves of them struck, as happened on a warm Sunday evening on April 11, 1965, it became impossible to give readers little more than highlights in the Monday paper. It was a time when the local television stations relied on a single weatherman to report what the National Weather Bureau was putting out, so that source was no better than what we were receiving. Their seven and eight-person weather teams are relatively new.

April 11 was Palm Sunday and at 70-degrees was uncommonly warm.

As city editor, I got a telephone call at home from Don Herring, who was running the city desk that Sunday. It was about 6 o'clock. He said there was a report of a tornado north of the city, but he said he thought he had enough help to cover the story. But a few minutes later he called again with sketchy reports about other tornadoes throughout the state. So I drove to the paper unaware of just how devastating the tornadoes had become.

Newsroom staffs on Sundays always are thin, so it was frustrating to send a reporter to cover an area that had been hit only to learn that another place ten miles away had even more damage. There was no way *The Star* was going to adequately cover the Palm Sunday tornadoes with a limited Sunday staff. And our usual source of news, the city and state police and sheriff's departments, were too busy to talk or were unreachable because power and telephone lines were down. Most of our part-time correspondents couldn't be reached either, though a few managed to feed bits of information to our state desk and to the wire services, Associated Press and United Press International. But the reports were sketchy.

The tornadoes came in three waves between 5:45 pm and 8:20 pm. The first wave struck across northern Indiana. Another series roared across the north central part of the state near Lafayette, Crawfordsville and Lebanon. Then a mile-wide tornado leveled the town of Russiaville just north of Indianapolis and hit other towns south of Kokomo. Because the storms did not hit Indianapolis it was difficult at first to realize the immensity of the disaster. It was only later that we learned that 45 persons had been killed near Elkhart in the small town of Dunlap. Thirty-three of those killed were in the same trailer park.

On the northern periphery of Indianapolis, the twisters destroyed several small towns near Lebanon, Sheridan and Arcadia, in addition to the havoc caused in Russiaville.

In addition to leveling entire towns, the 11 tornadoes killed 137 persons and injured more than 1,700 in 20 counties. Throughout the Midwest that day 50 tornadoes killed 271 and injured more than 3,000.

We didn't learn the extent of the death and damage for several days. Our initial coverage for the Monday morning paper was superficial, though the headlines promised more than we delivered. We continued to receive reports about damage and death in some of the more remote towns over the next few days. It got to be more of the same until interest waned and the press moved on to other topics. We didn't bother to wrap it up in a single story. In general, coverage of those tornadoes was not something the press could brag about. But six weeks later the UPI came out with a series of stories that tried to tell the entire story. It was valuable for the record, but a little too late as news.

¤

25 • An Interview in Paris

One night in the winter of 1952 I was drinking beer with a friend who came up with a preposterous suggestion:

"Why don't we take a leave of absence from our jobs and tour Europe?"

"Oh sure," I said. "Great idea, but what will we do for money? How would we travel around when we got there?" I had a dozen other reasons why the proposal was ridiculous.

But the friend, Tom Jordan, had given his proposal some thought. He'd done his research. He said we'd use our meager savings, borrow the rest, buy a car in England, bring it home, sell it at a profit and pay off the loans. The timing was right, too: the dollar was going a long way in post-war Europe. After the third beer, I was on his side, but I knew that ideas that blossomed at midnight usually wilted in the morning. This one didn't, and I think it was one of the two most significant decisions (second to marriage) I'd make in a lifetime of grappling with decisions.

I was a novice reporter so I reasoned that the paper wouldn't suffer from my absence. When I asked for a three-month leave, the city editor, Lowell Parker, thought the trip was a great idea. He said he envied us. Tom had arranged to take a leave from his job as director of the Catholic Youth Organization. My brother Nick agreed to provide me a loan—and suddenly we were in the planning stage.

Tom Jordan (l) and I were the proud owners of an MG TD ready for our 11-country tour.

Tom spent days devising an itinerary and arranging passage on a French liner, the *Liberte,* for a five-day crossing. We arranged to buy a car when we landed in England. That car—a beautiful new dark green MG-TD —took us through 11 countries. It was the key to a successful tour. The car cost $1,600. Three months later we brought it back with us on the *United States*, the liner that was making its return to the states on a record-setting maiden voyage. The liner crossed the Atlantic in three and a half days. It cost us $300 to bring the car with us, and we sold it for the same amount we paid for it—$1,600. It helped to pay off our loans.

I promised Parker I would send an occasional feature story, but not to count on any blockbusters. But there was one story I wanted to get in Paris. It was an interview with one of my literary idols, Janet Flanner, who wrote a fortnightly "Letter From Paris" under the penname, Genet, for *The New Yorker* magazine.

She would be a natural for a profile for the paper, I thought, because she had grown up in Indianapolis, and was the daughter of Frank Flanner, co-founder of the Flanner & Buchanan mortuaries. I'd heard that she had been eager to sever her ties to the city and to the family business when she left the city when she was 26. But I did not know that she had gotten her start in journalism at *The Star*, and that she became the nation's first newspaper movie critic when she worked for the paper in 1917 and 1918.

She had been living in Paris for three decades turning out her column almost from the year *The New Yorker* was founded in 1925. Her dispatches on the political, cultural and lifestyle scenes in Paris—all carefully researched and written with a distinct style that other writers on the magazine adopted—had made her one of the magazine's most admired writers. In her years in Paris in the twenties and thirties she had been part of the Left Bank group of artists and writers that included Picasso, Hemingway, Fitzgerald and Gertrude Stein.

I envied her life in Paris and admired her *New Yorker* letters, and regarded the magazine almost with awe. So I boldly wrote to her that I wished to interview her, and told her I would call when I arrived in Paris. My hopes were thin.

Tom and I had just settled in for a week's stay in Paris, our first stop after England. We had rented a room in the Hotel Diamond, a flophouse on the Rue Dunkerque. The dark and dreary room was lit by a single 40-watt bulb with a pull chain hanging from the ceiling. But it was cheap, a dollar a night, as I remember. The dingy room mattered little to us, though.

We were in Paris, driving a brand new MG up and down the Champs Elysees with a pair of French-Canadian lasses—Michelle and Micheline, who were fluent in French and knowledgeable about the city's museums and churches and, of course, the bistros. Tom had met Micheline on the ship, and she told him that she was planning to team up with her friend Michelle in Paris, so let's get together. Good idea.

After a few days in Paris, I managed to conquer a Parisian telephone and reached Miss Flanner at the Hotel Continental where she was living. She was hazy about me when I called but finally remembered my letter when I mentioned *The Star*. She wasn't gushing over my call but she did agree to give me a little time if I would come to her hotel at 10 o'clock the following morning.

At the appointed time, I entered the hotel and proceeded to her room. I knocked on the door. No response. I waited and knocked again. Finally, I heard a woman with a smoker's voice bark, "Who is it?" I told her my name and she opened the door, still wearing her robe.

"Why didn't you call up from the desk?" she snapped. "You can't just barge in here."

I mumbled some apology and she relented, invited me in, and told me to have a seat while she got dressed.

She was 60 years old, small, somewhat mannish with a severe hairdo. She appeared nervous and spoke rapidly, a woman in a hurry. I learned later that she had always lived in hotel rooms in Paris. From my prior research, I learned that she had married an Indiana banker in 1920 and after considerable travel settled in Paris in 1922. The marriage didn't last and Flanner engaged in lesbian relationships the rest of her life.

The interview moved along smoothly because I asked no difficult questions about her personal life, but she did bristle when asked about her relationship with the Flanner family of morticians.

"For Christ's sake, don't mention that," she said.

I left with what I thought was enough information for a decent profile, though later I wished that I had asked about her method of researching and writing her columns. I was somewhat intimidated by the great lady and at that time I was no relentless reporter.

A couple of days later I received a letter addressed to Monsieur CONNOR at our hotel asking if she could see the story before it ran. She wrote that she had been burned once by granting an interview to a writer on the *New York Herald* in Paris. I agreed and sent her the copy a few weeks later.

She made some minor changes and added a clarification about her work as the nation's first movie critic when she worked at *The Star* in her mid-twenties. In a note accompanying the copy, she wrote, "It was an intelligent decision for Frank Tarkington Baker (*The Star's* drama critic) to treat movies, though newcomers, as important." At that time movies were aimed at juveniles and uncultured adults, she said.

Baker assigned her to review the first movie for the paper. It was Chaplin's *The Kid*.

"Imagine, I wrote three-quarters of a column and was thrilled when the movie house republished excerpts of it," she wrote.

Her note also included a plea: "Please when you copy your piece as now you must, poor man, ask your editor to leave out the family business connections as we women left in the family would like to forget it." I obliged.

Janet Flanner wrote under the penname "Genet" for The New Yorker *magazine.*

I heard from her again after I sent her a copy of the *Star Magazine* that carried the story. She responded with a compliment that any young reporter would have cherished—"And a very nice, very well-constructed overall piece it is on me." Then she noted that the Circle Theater "was certainly the first luxury movie house, built to be that & nothing else, with first rising-and-falling platform for the orchestra on which they played, when up, big operatic or symphonic solo numbers, very well too. They were first at that too, the inclusion of good if popular classic music as a solo feature of the program."

I have saved the letters and the copy as she edited it.

She said that in all the time that she had been writing for *The New Yorker*, she still hadn't deciphered her pen name, "Genet," which turned up several years earlier.

"I looked up the French meanings and found three, none of which mattered," she wrote. "Ross [Harold Ross, founder of the magazine] never told me what it meant. Frankly, I think he thought it was a nice French way of spelling Janet."

She said his only instruction when she signed on with the magazine was, "Don't write about France. Write about the French."

Most of her friends in those early years in Paris were writers, artists, poets and journalists. They gathered at sidewalk cafes and bistros with their coffee or martinis, depending upon the time of day. All were somewhat contemptuous of Americans.

In her letters from Paris she wrote of French politics, art, theater and lifestyles. Realizing that she could not compete with daily newspapers, she used the "letter" formula, which didn't deal with breaking news but rather with the effect it had on the French.

In a biography titled *Genet,* the author, Brenda Wineapple, wrote that "Janet consistently described Indiana as a hateful place, with its bourgeois standards, its lack of beauty, and its elongated flat spaces."

When she reminded me more than once in our dealings to not mention her connection to the source of the family's fortune, the Flanner & Buchanan mortuaries, I had not known then that her father had committed suicide when Janet was 20 years old. It became a local scandal that Janet said she would remember for the rest of her life, Wineapple wrote.

It happened on February 17, 1912. Flanner, then 58, bought an assortment of drugs at various drug stores and went into the chapel of the firm's new mortuary at 320 North Illinois Street. He made a mixture of prussic acid, strychnine, carbolic acid and morphine and mixed it in a cup and drank it. Paul Buchanan, his brother-in-law and partner, found him on a davenport in the chapel 30 minutes later.

Flanner had been a community leader. The front page account of his death in *The News* mentioned that he had founded Flanner Guild, "which has for its object settlement and education work of the colored people of the city." It was the forerunner of Flanner House, which still exists.

Janet may have gotten her distaste for the business from her mother. There was talk that she had inadvertently pushed her husband into suicide because she was ashamed of his occupation. But the story in *The News* said her father had been in ill health for a year and was despondent. Janet was listed as Janette, one of his three surviving daughters.

Flanner continued to write her "Letter From Paris" for another 20 years after I met her. She also wrote several books, one of which brought her the National Book Award in 1966. It was for the first part of her two-volume *Paris Journal* (1965-71). By then she was being called "America's Tocqueville."

She died in 1978 at age 86.

¤

26 • Monsters on the Loose

Sundays in the newsroom could be tedious and boring. Until 5 p.m., when the copy desk crew arrived, the place was occupied by a half dozen staffers—an assistant city editor, a state editor, wire editor, perhaps three reporters and a fourth reporter stationed at police headquarters. All of the other departments in the building were dark.

And most of the city was quiet with little going on that could be considered newsworthy. Our hopes rested with the police reporter for coming up with a story that developed overnight—a murder, an auto accident, or a ruckus at one of the city's taverns. It was why Monday's front page carried 96-point headline streamers screaming "Two Die In Indo-China," or "Coup in Madagascar," stories that might warrant two paragraphs on the classified page any other day of the week.

Richard Randolph Roberts' formidable appearance was surpassed by his many memorable stories and antics.

There were Sundays when we even welcomed calls from funeral homes with information for obituaries. But we could usually count on Richard Randolph Roberts to come up with an offbeat story when he was manning the state desk. During the summer someone somewhere in the state would spot a monster of some kind. The Beast of Busco showed up in Churubusco near Fort Wayne in the late 1940s. It looked like a dinosaur when it stuck its head out of the water, but the best guess was that it was a giant turtle. Naturalists decided the little green men seen in Southern Indiana were probably tree frogs. Big Foot brought the curious to the banks of the Ohio River in the sixties.

So Roberts was ready when a correspondent called in on a Sunday in June, 1960, to report that people were showing up at a farm in eastern Indiana to get a look at a monster. He grilled the correspondent, turned to his typewriter and came up with the Monster of Craig's Well. The headline on the story on page one announced "Eerie Monster Inhabits Farm Well." The story read:

Lynn, Ind. (Spl.) — An ever-widening circle of Eastern In-

> diana was buzzing—and shuddering— last night over the mystery of Craig's Well.
>
> The eerie, mushroom-colored beast, which has a dome-shaped head with two bulbous, staring eyes on top, and eight powerful flailing tentacles as long as a man's arm, with gray, lobster-type claws on two ends, lurks in a cistern 12 feet deep and 10 feet in diameter on the Dan Craig farm.
>
> An ever-growing stream of visitors anxious to determine what The Thing is and where it came from has been surrounding the monster's lair on Craig's farm on the Randolph County line four miles south of Lynn.
>
> They are hampered in their views because the mouth of the cistern is only two feet across. The cistern itself is shaped like a giant, subterranean milk bottle and the beast often stalks at the bottom.
>
> To stay on the safe side, since he has a wife and four young children, Craig keeps the spooky cistern covered.
>
> The 56-year-old, 200-pound Craig, a tree removal contractor, first saw The Thing sloshing around in the murky depths of the well about a year ago.
>
> For a while, the monster's existence was kept relatively secret. Last Saturday, Craig's curiosity got the best of him. He pumped the well dry.
>
> The bottom was covered with timber, sticks and scrap metal. Craig and other watchers gazed fascinated as the monster crawled up onto the timbers, but in the dark gloom, it was hard to see.
>
> A farmer lowered a fish on a string and pulled it up awhile later, slashed to ribbons. He took it home and fed it to his cat. Fifteen minutes later the cat died.
>
> Craig thought someone brought it back from the tropics when it was small and when it got bigger looked for a place to get rid of it and picked Craig's well.

The next day Roberts kept the mystery alive with another story reporting that 52 carloads of "bug-eyed thrill seekers disrupted the quiet of Dan Craig's farm to get a peek at the eerie beast."

After four days the story drifted to an inside page and then died. The monster turned out to be an old tire and a length of garden hose.

If the Sundays produced little or no news, Dick ground out parodies for the entertainment of co-workers. Or he'd dash off a nagging letter to the editor that would generate angry responses. Typical was one complaining about women bringing crying infants to the supermarket.

On one slow Sunday he fed a roll of teletype paper into his typewriter and typed the names of all of the reporters and editors and photographers he could remember who had been hired since he had started there several years earlier. The list was some 50 feet long, extending down the hallway. You had to ask if *The Star* was training journalists for the nation's newspapers or was low pay driving them out the door.

Most of the staff enjoyed or, at least, tolerated Roberts's eccentricities. One who didn't was rewriteman Leon Russell, a middle-aged bachelor who had two interests—his large collection of paperback novels and a complete set of Gilbert and Sullivan recordings.

A fastidious sort, he lined up his pencils and paper at the start of each shift and waited for the police reporter to phone him with information about any crimes and calamities worth noting. Leon despised the telephone and rock 'n roll music.

When the paper's promotion department thought that Musak would give the place some class, it was installed throughout the building except in the newsrooms of the two papers. One evening Dick told Leon that he had learned that the canned music was to be fed into the newsrooms after all. An angry Leon quickly vowed that he would quit if it happened.

So the next day, a lazy Sunday, Roberts placed a record player in the artist's shack in a corner of the newsroom. When he saw Leon lumbering down the hall at 5 o'clock, he turned the phonograph at full volume and out blared a particularly irritating rock 'n roll number. Leon couldn't believe it was happening but a reporter told him that there was an announcement about the change on the bulletin board. Leon raced to the bulletin board, read the bogus announcement and then smashed his fist through the board. He was heading for the door when he was told it was all a gag, but he steamed for the rest of the night, and nursed a sore hand for several days.

Roberts labeled a drawer in a file cabinet "Crimea War File—Sevastopol." Jammed in it were books, a slab of salami, a blackjack, some canned goods, a coffee maker, a telescope, magazines and some of his manuscripts. He carried a brief case similarly laden.

Dick was brought up in a liberal Democrat home in Fort Wayne where his father, soft-spoken Frank Roberts, was longtime editor of the *Fort Wayne Journal-Gazette*, and his mother, Bessie Keeran Roberts, was an historian and one time an internationally syndicated newspaper columnist. The couple hosted dinners at their home for many writers including Carl Sandburg, Vachel Lindsay, Claude Bowers, and Ross Lockridge. Dick's father loved literature and could quote pages of writings of Shakespeare, Milton, Plato and others and apply the quotations to a subject at hand. He reportedly could also quote verbatim speeches of politicians and others, such as Clarence Darrow, that he had heard as a boy. He covered many of the Democratic conventions in the twenties and thirties where he became friends with William Allen White and H. L. Mencken.

His son was well educated and well read, and, much like his father, able to recall facts from history, literature, philosophy and economics. He was also a fitness addict, jogging two to four miles almost daily well into his 80s. Short, solidly built, he gave an impression of being aggressive with his deep, raspy voice, but he actually was a gentle and considerate person.

As he aged, he rejected liberalism and became an archconservative, saying he voted for Disraeli in the last election. In his last years at the paper, Dick was an editorial writer. His views fitted in with the paper's conservative stance. And his editorials were vivid and colorful, especially when he wrote about the change in seasons. He had difficulty working with a tall, stout Britisher who was hired as an editorial writer. Dick said the man had a fixation that the national debt was at the bottom of every social ill in the country. "If he wrote an editorial about the raping of five girls," Roberts said, "he would add that it was simply a manifestation of the social crisis brought on by the skyrocketing national debt."

Dick moved to Florida after retiring but he would write an occasional editorial for the paper. I received an e-mail message from him concerning the treatment of one of his Indian summer editorials. It read:

> A girl named Wolf (that would be Judy) on the copy desk, to be referred to hereafter as the Wolf Girl, phoned to request that the title of the editorial be changed from Injun Summer to Indian Summer because "Injun" might be considered derisive. I told her to go ahead and change it if it would make her happy but that I thought it was silly, hypersensitive, hypercritical and

> hyperbolic and that the current mass neurotic concern over human nomenclature amounted to walking around with chips on both shoulders and is turning the country into a nation of crybabies and wimps.

Dick has concluded that the world is a mess and he blames a lot of its troubles on today's press. When I am not listening to his diatribes over the phone, I am getting e-mails like this one I received a couple of years ago.

> You mentioned a book on what b.s. purveyors most scribes/scribblers/news media are today. Winchell et al. were saints compared to most of the greenass frauds and propagandists in the "journalism"/brainwashing racket today — cutie Couric and all those babes who stick out their boobs and pull up their skirts and "explain" why the camel humpers are the good guys and the Jews are the bad guys for going after them when they blow up kids in restaurants and use their own children as bomber-murders. The whole history and scene are cases of massive distortion, lies, b. s. and fraud. The goddam Muslim nations had endless opportunities to give land and refuge to the Palestinians for their own country. The "camps" are festering sores intended to do exactly what they had done and are doing: churn up hatred and violence without end until all of the Jews are dead. After Hitler, no sane person can blame the Jews for anything they do to blast their attackers and hold their own ground.

And here was his take on stories about the Catholic priests sex scandal:

> The Catholic priest "molesting" stories are distorted, mishandled and full of crap, for the most part. I think a lot of the "victims" are bullshit artists and shakedown players looking for unmerited sympathy and payoffs. If they were in their teens and so horribly affected by having their erotic zones played with, why the hell didn't they jump out of bed and run and deck the poor priests who were "molesting" them. I think the "victims" are phonies. Some guy was quoted today (I missed his name,

unfortunately) as saying he would have taken a baseball bat to those self-designated victims who had their fun and then blossomed into publicity hounds. Of course, turning this sexcapade flurry into massive moral collapse fits into the nihilists' game of wrecking and befouling all of the elements of the past that helped hold society together and kept it from turning into a revival of Sodom and Gomorrah, on a massively bigger scale, despite the obvious ironies—just as the U. S. military and its adjuncts kept the goddam camel humpers from blowing up the White House and Congress and buildings, power grids, ports and port cities, military bases and populations all over the country. Those bastards are nuts. They always have been. And they want to destroy Western civilization, which, decadent as it is, is Paradise compared to life in those shitty Asian and African hell-holes, which are not even fit for pigs and goats.

Put that in your pipe and smoke it.
Writing is fun, isn't it?

¤

27 • We're Entertained

Richard Randolph Roberts frequently entertained co-workers on those slow Sundays with poems and parodies.

To note the fall season in Brown County, he wrote:

> Thousands of whiskey-besotted Midwestern businessmen were careening in their Cadillacs toward Brown County last night, their secretaries at their sides, a shack job in a tourist cabin their destination, after telling their wives, 'Wanna run down looka them red leaves.

Dick let his imagination run free when turning out bogus news items like this one:

> Gobbler's Nob, Ind. (Spl.)—State Police last night were seeking a tall dark man wanted for shooting a beautiful blonde nightclub singer between Twin Peaks and Hell's Hollow.
>
> The curvaceous singer, Patsy Pinkus, 18 years old, Gobbler's Nob, was in beastly shape at Crumpacker Memorial Hospital suffering a punctured poitrine.
>
> Her assailant, whom she named as John Wilkes Booth Hamburger, 30, Pinhook, was being pursued through Hobblemeyer Forest by bloodhounds.
>
> She charged Hamburger, a retired beggar, with ripping off her clothes in an effort to force his attentions on her, then shooting her with a North Korean burp gun when she blushed.

When the police reporter was unable to come up with a gruesome murder for Monday's edition, Dick dreamed up this one for the staff's benefit:

> Nails Grogan, 49 years old, 9 Roundhouse Alley, prominent Indianapolis cutthroat, died unexpectedly yesterday in a fashionable North Side gutter.
>
> Death was ascribed to complications and natural causes. Five bullet holes were found in Grogan's head and several more slugs had penetrated his heart, lungs and abdomen.
>
> Grogan, who achieved statewide fame through his activities as a dope peddler, card shark, finger man and heist expert, rose from obscurity in a humble Haughville neighborhood.
>
> He was one of fourteen children who chalked up more spectacular criminal records than members of any other single Hoosier family.

> One of his brothers, Rufus, won wide attention at Columbia University where his brain was put on display in a bottle of formaldehyde following electrocution for ravishing and murdering a 99-year-old grandmother.
>
> Another made headlines for his leading role in the torture death of a Martinsville tot.
>
> Others were prominent in bigamy, buggery, simony, arson, mayhem and holdup circles.
>
> Grogan was a member of the Ku Klux Klan, the Black Legion, the Knights of the White Camelia, the Silver Shirts, and the International Brotherhood of Thieves, Cutpurses and Second Story Men. He was a charter member and onetime president of the Cesspool Society and was listed in Slutweiler's Encyclopedia of Underworld Kingpins.
>
> Funeral services will be at midnight Saturday at the Indianapolis Sewage Disposal Plant. The body is lying in state at the City Morgue. Burial will be in Potter's Field.
>
> Survivors are the most unsavory lots of thugs, brigands, hoodlums and blackguards this side of the gates of hell.

And then there was the coroner's convention:

> Coroners from throughout the nation will assemble in Los Angeles Aug. 22 to 23 to select Miss Autopsy of 1951, "The Body Any Coroner Would Like to Examine."
>
> The winner among 100 comely beauties will be crowned "Queen of the Coroners," and will receive a ticket entitling her to free embalming, casket, burial service and graveyard plot.
>
> The coronation will take place Friday in the Bustline Patio of the Biltmore Hotel.
>
> Coroner A. Sharpe Scalpel of Coffin Gulch, N. D., will be master of ceremonies.
>
> Committee for the event will include Dr. M. D. Suture, Bloodbank, Me., Dr. James Hemostat, Merthiolate, Ala., Dr. Lister D. Embolism, Carcinoma, Ark., and Coroner Wasserman J. Flunk, Clapps, Miss.

Dick enjoyed making fun of our sister paper, *The News*, and in particular its Herman Hoglebogle column. Herman, a cartoon character, first showed up in *The News* in 1950. He was featured in one of those columns designed to help readers solve their problems by calling on Herman for advice. Herman, a tireless campaigner for the public's good, was big on pointing out traffic hazards and warning readers about pitfalls awaiting them on the city's streets. Here's how Dick would have written a Hoglebogle story:

> While impish little Herman Hoglebogle snickered and pointed his finger in the shadows, jaywalking Mrs. Lucinda Potholder, 82, 1212 Grommet Ave., was hurled heavily to the hard concrete by a passing 15-ton tractor-trailer.
>
> Had Mrs. Potholder heeded Hoglebogle's warnings, she might be alive today, warming to the sun's dawning, listening to the robin's twitter, depositing taffy apples, fudge, gumdrops, oranges, raisin cookies, devil's food cake, lukimi, Turkish Delight and margepin in the sticky little palms of the kids in the neighborhood, who she could not bear, in her lovable generosity, to see go hungry; yes, she would be with her noted green thumb gingerly prompting tulips, after a long winter of quiescence, to poke their many-colored little buds into the spring air; scattering bread crumbs for the wrens and knitting afghans for the Air Force.
>
> Alas, she won't. She disregarded Herman Hoglebogle. She is no more.
>
> Fifteen tons of cruel, hard steel hurtled through the dark intersection of Muck Boulevard and Gomorrah Street, driven by Alphonso McCracken, 32, Pumpkin Corners, owned by the Bittersweet Diaper Laundry Machinery Company Inc. of Crapulent Heights, Idaho.
>
> It hit Mrs. Potholder.
>
> It broke her back.
>
> In five places.
>
> It crushed her skull.
>
> It snapped her poor old legs.
>
> It fractured her sacroiliac.
>
> It ruptured her spleen
>
> It dislocated her pelvis.
>
> It fragmented her collarbone.

It exploded her bladder.
It flooded her Islands of Langerhans.
It slipped her discs.
It abraded her mons veneris.
It punctured her herpineal gland.
It pierced her coccyx.
It pulverized her femur, tibula and fibula.
It battered her hatches.

In short, because she didn't listen to Herman Hoglebogle, Mrs. Potholder is a real gone old lady, gone all the way – to her reward – the reward of all jaywalkers.

McCracken, the driver, was not held.

Funeral services for Mrs. Potholder, who was born in Hicksville, O., but didn't begin to live until she came to Indianapolis in 1898, will be held at 2:30 p. m. tomorrow at the P. H. Brindelbone North Hough Street Temple of Eternal Peace. Burial will be in Sour Mash Cemetery.

There are no immediate survivors.

Pay attention to Hoglebogle.

¤

28 • An Appeal For Help

While *The News's* Herman Hoglebogle had been handing out advice to readers for nearly a quarter of a century, we decided to start our own column in the 1970s. It was designed to give readers a place to go for advice and assistance and a place to air their beefs. We called it Intercom. While it lasted, the column generated about 150 letters a week. Here are two letters addressed to Intercom in 1977. They came from a woman living in southern Indiana in the town of Loogootee. I guess we can say that it was written in a rural Indiana "stream of consciousness" style. It played hell with my spellchecker. I've changed the names in the plea. It read:

> I was invited to a wedinganaversity party and I was to bring kentucky fried chicken I bough 21,pc, and "Jane Doe," daughter jayne bough 21,pc, of ky chicken pint liver , daughter "Mary Jones" bough 21,pc, ky chicken and 1 pint liver gizards and we all got so sick we threw up and had the runnenoff so bad we were so sick we wished were ded we were throwen up and had the runnen off for 4 days and "Mary Jones" had to go to the dr to get medicun for all of our direa we were so sick "Emma Smith" works at a nersen home and the nerses bough chicken the same day and they all got sick like us sicker than dogs the party was sept 27,75 and I rote ky fried chicken restrent at jasper ind 47546 and I never got a word and at "Mary Jones"s daughter school the neice of the manager of ky fried chicken restrant had a leter and red it at school that was suposed to be the same leter I was to get and never got it stated if I didnt like the chicken to not by any more from them "Jane Doe" went to the restrant and complained to the manager and she would not do nothing about it would not give here money back I bough a nother snack pack sense that for here mother 3 pc chicken ,1, mashpotatoes, 1role, 1,slaw , gravey on potatoes it made her sick like the party chicken and she eats chicken all the time nen had to miss work cause they were sick for all the chicken we got those to time a we spent $30,00 for it and was so sickening I rote them the other day to and told them the reason I rote I didn't want to make a big stink at the store never got a word can you help me.

We did—sort of.

We notified the KFC Corporation home office at Louisville and sent along a copy of the letter. The corporation sent her a gift certificate worth $8 and we received a letter explaining the sanitation procedures taken at each of the restaurants. We were further informed that the manager of the Jasper restaurant told the home office that 364 chickens were cooked on the day in question without a single other report of illness.

We later heard from the same woman with another complaint. This one read:

> I got whisker lickens cat food and sent 6, proofs to the company to get to hanging planters and never got them I rote them to or more tims and never got a word and then I got more papers and sent them in and told them they still owed me to hanging planters , and I got the last to I ordered and not the ones they owed me long time if they dony want to send the planters th ey can send ,e $1.00 they got now to send out for the same amou nt of proof percipes , it to whisker licking planter. p.o.box 9992, st, paul minn, 55199. ____ ____and _____ ____ _, ______ _____ , saced wate sircles from purnia cat chow and they wont send the coupons to us at all "Emma Slagle" got 6.22 oz boxes coupons and 1, 4, lbs coupon comen and never got and I rote for here and they wont answer me and she rote to and don't do any good as her cat is a simeas and cant eat much kind only cat chow in the blue sack and i got 4.4 lbs sac ls and 7.22 oz box comen and cant get them to send them to me at all I keep complainen for them and it don't do any good and I and tired of riten for them and "Lily Jones" got 3, 3 big sacks coupons com n she sent the coupons in to they send here a coupon for 22 oz not the big sack were are tired of saven the coupon for nothing Evelyn ….. _______ ______all ours address the same of the three ladeys.

We passed on this one.

¤

29 • Murder On The Ocean

I've always felt that Mary Jordan deserved more than to end up as little more than a footnote in a bizarre tragedy that happened in Bahamian waters 45 years ago.

When I knew Mary a half century ago she and I shared one of those old wooden typewriter desks jammed into the city room at *The Star*. In those days reporters were usually hired by how they registered with the city editor. In Mary's case, I'm guessing that Lowell Parker, the city editor, hired her because she was personable and attractive, and had a modicum of journalism training. She was a pleasant addition to a newsroom staffed with old-timers who had held the paper together during the war.

That would have been in late 1952. Mary had graduated a few months earlier from Butler University where she had been a popular campus leader; president of the swimming club, editor of *The Butler Collegian*, the student newspaper, and active in the Delta Delta Delta sorority.

"Everybody loved Mary," Bill Sylvester recalled. He had dated her when they were students at Butler. Bill was the star quarterback on the football team and later football coach and athletic director at the university. "She was athletic, an outstanding swimmer. Mary was involved in all kinds of campus activities. She was just an all-around fun person," he remembered.

Mary fitted in well at the paper. As a cub reporter, she wrote her share of obituaries and rewrote some of the news releases that poured in with each mail delivery. I'm sure she envisioned the job as the first step in an exciting career in journalism, but she didn't complain about her mundane duties, so when Parker needed someone to fill in as church editor, he tapped Mary. It was a step up but a short one. Most of the work entailed writing one and two-paragraph shorts for the Saturday church page; a relatively easy way for Mary to earn a $45 weekly paycheck. She was usually out of the City Room by 5 o'clock—about the time I was coming in from City Hall to write about whatever the mayor or one of his department heads had fed me that day.

Mary used two of the drawers in the desk we shared and I used the third one. We sometimes left notes to each other in the Royal typewriter that sat in the well of the desk. Most were about calls for the other person, but occasionally Mary's sense of humor turned up. One evening a note greeted me—"Stay Out of My Drawers." It wasn't the come-on that it seemed to be; it was a response to Parker's placing a copy of Sexology magazine in her desk drawer.

Typing church notes didn't satisfy Mary's adventurous spirit, so she left after a year and a half to take a job as an airline stewardess, a job coveted in those years by young women looking for adventure, travel and romance. She was based in Los Angeles.

Mary's reputation for playing practical jokes backfired on her when she returned home in August of 1955 to marry a chiropractic student named Russell Smith.

Margaret (Maggie) Jordan Bromund, who sat next to Mary through four years at the old Thomas Carr Howe High School, recalled that during the wedding reception at the Tri Delt house at Butler, she and some of Mary's friends threw Mary's trousseau from the second-story window, and some of the clothes got snagged in a tree. If that wasn't enough, Mary's older brother and some of his friends shanghaied Mary, drove her away from the reception, and dropped her off at a golf course.

"She thought it was all great fun," Bromund said.

With Mary often away on extended airline flights, she and her husband drifted apart and the marriage ended after two years.

The day she left *The Star* in 1954 was the last I heard of Mary until a November afternoon in 1961 when a bulletin came into the newsroom about a boating accident in the Atlantic Ocean 50 miles northwest of Nassau. The report said a family of five and the wife of the captain were lost when the boat sank during a sudden squall. The sole survivor was Julian Harvey, the captain of the 60-foot ketch, the *Bluebelle*, that operated as a chartered cruise boat in the Caribbean. Harvey had been adrift in a 10-foot dinghy for 14 hours before being rescued by a tanker.

A few hours after the story broke someone called the city desk to report that Harvey's wife was Mary Jordan, the same Mary Jordan who had worked at *The Star*.

News accounts of the tragedy over the next few days mentioned Mary only in passing. They were focused on the Arthur Duperrault family of Green Bay, Wisconsin, who, Harvey told authorities, were lost when the *Bluebelle* sank. The shocker came three days after the *Bluebelle* sank when an 11-year-old girl was spotted drifting in the Atlantic on a small life raft. Baked by the sun and dehydrated after 82 hours adrift, the child sank into a two-day coma after telling her rescuers that she was Terry Jo Duperrault.

Harvey learned of her rescue while being questioned by Coast Guard officials who had become skeptical of his account, but Harvey had a good reputation in boating circles, and search teams had found no trace of the boat or of those aboard. When informed of the child's rescue, Harvey said, "Isn't that wonderful," but he appeared shaken. Minutes later he left the room where he and the boat's owner were being questioned. The next day he rented a room in a Miami motel under the name John Monroe and slashed his thigh, wrists and throat with a razor. He had finger painted the wall with his blood. In a suicide note addressed to a friend in Miami, Harvey wrote: "I was tired and nervous. I couldn't stand it any longer." There was no mention of the tragedy.

Mary and Harvey had been married only four months. It was her second marriage, his fifth. They had met in Miami and had planned to marry in early summer of 1961, but they quarreled a few days before the wedding and called it off. Friends said Mary was devastated and she finally made the overture to reconcile. They were married in Tijuana, Mexico, on July 26. She was 33, he 45. Friends said Mary was ecstatic about her romance with Harvey, a rugged and handsome former Powers model and war hero, but they had also heard that the couple continued to quarrel after they were married.

The *Bluebelle's* owner was Howard S. Pegg, a swimming pool contractor in Hollywood, Florida. The craft was built in 1928 as a racing boat but had been redesigned and was being chartered as a cruise boat. A month before it sank, Pegg hired Harvey as skipper of the boat, and he arranged for Harvey and Mary to live on it and take tourists on cruises.

Living on a boat, sailing in the Caribbean and writing short stories was the sort of Hemingway life that would have appealed to Mary. She had submitted a script for a television drama series and been encouraged to continue writing. A novel was her ultimate goal.

I wondered later if Mary knew much about Harvey before she married him. He had enrolled at Purdue University in 1940 and enlisted in the Army Air Corps a year later. He returned to Purdue and was graduated in 1948 with a degree in mechanical engineering. Harvey as a war hero surely impressed Mary. He had flown 29 bomber missions in World War II and 114 fighter missions in Korea and earned 12 decorations. He became a test pilot and retired as a lieutenant colonel about a year before they were married.

But I wondered if Mary knew that Harvey had at least four previous wives, perhaps more. And that the second of those wives and her mother drowned in 1949 in a Florida bayou after Harvey drove a car into a bridge railing on a rain-swept highway near Eglin Air Force Base, and that he had leaped to safety before it tore out 30 feet of bridge railing and then dropped into the water?

There were other blots on Harvey's unrevealed resume that Mary may have missed, including three airplane crashes during his 17 years in service.

I wondered, too, if she was aware that his 60-foot auxiliary sailboat sank in Chesapeake Bay in 1956 when it hit the hull of a submerged but clearly marked battleship, and that he subsequently collected $14,258 in damages from the U. S. government. Or that he lost another craft under his command two years later when the 80-foot *Valiant* caught fire and sank off the coast of Cuba.

And did she know that two months before the *Bluebelle* went down that Harvey was broke; yet he took out a $20,000 double indemnity insurance policy on her life, listing himself as sole beneficiary?

When the Duperrault family left their home in Green Bay, Wisconsin, it was the plan of 41-year-old Arthur Duperrault to purchase a sailboat and cruise in Caribbean waters with his family for three months. Duperrault and his wife, Jean, 38, took their children—Brian, 14, Terry Jo, 11, and Rene, 7—out of school and headed south on October 13, 1961.

Duperrault was well known in Green Bay. A successful optometrist, he was a leader in church and civic affairs and one of the state's top handball players. Both he and his wife were outstanding golfers.

Duperrault spent nearly a month in Florida shopping for a boat without success, so he decided to charter the *Bluebelle* for a week's cruise in the Bahamas. They sailed out of Fort Lauderdale on November 8. Five days out and the boat sank in deep water 120 miles northeast of Miami. There were no radio calls for help.

Fourteen hours later Harvey was rescued by a tanker, the *Gulf Lion*. With him in a 10-foot dinghy was the body of 7-year-old Rene who had drowned.

At Coast Guard hearings the next day, Harvey told a harrowing tale. He said the *Bluebelle* was hit by a sudden squall about 11 o'clock on the previous Sunday night. The mainmast broke and crashed into the hull, and then the mizzenmast fell among the occupants in the cockpit, injuring some of them. Harvey said he tended to the injured and went to the forecastle to get a pair of cable cutters. When he emerged, he said, he saw fire spreading across the deck, so he went to the main cabin to get fire extinguishers. But they had little effect on the fire. He said he discovered the mainmast had opened a hole in the boat and within 15 minutes the *Bluebelle* sank. He said he was able to get the dinghy into the water but was unable to locate his wife or the passengers who had jumped overboard, but he did see Rene floating in the water. He pulled her into the dinghy and gave her artificial respiration without success.

But Terry Jo told authorities a different story after she came out of a two-day coma. Questioned by Coast Guard and FBI officials in her heavily guarded hospital room, she said she saw no fire and the mainmast was leaning but wasn't broken. There was a light rain that night but no squall, she said.

She said she was awakened when she heard screaming, stomping and running noises. She heard her brother yelling, "Help, Daddy, help." She got out of her bunk and went to the central cabin where she saw her mother and brother lying on the floor. They were not moving and there was blood around them. She raced up on the deck and saw more blood there. No one was steering the boat, and when Harvey saw her, she said, he shoved her down the stairs and told her to get back in her room. She said she never saw her father, Rene, or Mary anytime after she was awakened.

A short time later, she said, Harvey came into her room holding what she thought could have been a rifle. She said he terrified her. He stared at her and then turned and left.

With water rising to the level of her mattress, Terry Jo said she left her room, and climbed the stairway to the main deck. Harvey told her the boat was sinking. Stranded on the sinking boat, she watched Harvey dive into the Atlantic and get on a 10-foot dinghy. She was left behind to become his final victim. But Harvey misjudged her. She spotted a small balsa raft tied to the roof of the deck's cabin, untied it, climbed aboard and floated clear as water washed over the deck.

Under a broiling sun for three days and four terrifying nights, she was able to stay aboard the tiny raft without food or water. The raft was so small that she had to curl into a fetal position to lie down. In the vast ocean, the white raft looked much like one of the thousands of whitecaps bobbing in the water.

After floating for 82 hours, she was rescued by crewmen on a Greek freighter. Near death from dehydration and exposure, the flaxen-haired girl was rushed by helicopter to Mercy Hospital in Miami. Before she sank into a two-day coma, she was able to mumble her name.

When rescued she was wearing pink slacks and a white blouse and no shoes. She said parrotfish nibbled at her toes through the ropes that crisscrossed the floor of the raft. At times she said she hallucinated, once thinking she saw an island and paddled toward it.

Five months after the *Bluebelle* went down the Coast Guard ruled that Harvey had murdered Mary and the Duperrault family and sank the boat. The principal motive cited by the Coast Guard was the double indemnity insurance policy on Mary's life. But was that enough of a motive for him to murder six people, including a wife of four months whom his friends said was "the girl of his dreams."

One investigator surmised that Harvey may have murdered Mary after one of their arguments, and when one of the Duperraults saw him do it, decided he had to murder all of them. Years later evidence pointed to another possible scenario: that Harvey was part of a botched drug smuggling scheme. A federal court document filed in 1998 charged that the boat owner, the late Harold Pegg, and his two sons were involved in a multi-million-dollar drug running operation. Terry Jo's father or brother may have witnessed an ocean rendezvous with another drug boat, which could have triggered the murders.

Was Julian Harvey evil or insane?

There will be no DNA tests on him, no exhuming of his body. In line with a wish he had left in a suicide note, Harvey's body, encased in a black bag, returned to the Atlantic from the fantail of a gleaming luxury yacht 10 miles from Miami a few days after his death. Standing at the port rail were two of his sons by two of his former wives.

It has always seemed ironic that all of the elements for a major American novel came together on that November night in 1961, but instead of writing the novel, Mary Jordan wound up as a minor character in an American tragedy.

And what memories does the lone survivor have of Mary and her husband and that night?

Even today she said she never detected any animosity between Harvey and her father, nor any between Mary and Harvey, during the five days they were aboard the *Bluebelle.*

"I just remember that Mrs. Harvey was warm and friendly," Terry Jo recalled. "She did the cooking and acted like a hostess. We were all having a good time. When we stopped at islands in the Bahamas, she and the captain stayed on the boat."

During the days Terry Jo spent in the hospital, she received gifts and letters of encouragement from people all over the world. The hospital staff treated her like royalty.

Terry Jo in the Miami Hospital.

It's been a long and often painful journey from that November night in 1961, but through it all she has tried to remain upbeat and optimistic. Eleven days after the *Bluebelle* sank, she returned to Wisconsin to live with her aunt and uncle, Ralph and Dottie Scheer, and their children in DePere near Green Bay. Despite being well treated, Terry Jo found it difficult to adjust to a new family in a new house in a new town. The Scheers, who became her guardians, effectively kept her sheltered from the media in all the years that she was in their care.

It wasn't until 20 years later that she talked publicly about the tragedy and how it had affected her life. Keith Goldschmidt of the *Green Bay Press-Gazette* interviewed her while she was living in West Berlin with her second husband who was serving in the U. S. Army. They were living there with their two children and her daughter by her first husband.

Of her 82 hours on the raft, she told Goldschmidt:

> I prayed a lot. I prayed to God to help me. I never said to save me or anything like that. I never had any doubts that I would be saved. I don't know if being an 11-year-old went through my mind or not. I just asked Him to help me. I never cried. I never thought of giving up, though. I saw planes and a few ships at night, and I'd try to paddle to them.

Life after the *Bluebelle* was often difficult, especially during her adolescence. She couldn't accept that her father, whom she idolized, was dead. She fantasized that he might have swum to an island and would show up one day.

Feeling the need to break away from her life in Green Bay, at 16 she enrolled in a girl's boarding school in Lake Forest, Illinois, but soon left. A year later she had a nervous breakdown and was under the care of a psychiatrist for a year, she said.

After graduating from high school, she enrolled at the University of Wisconsin-Stevens Point and spent a summer session in Spain, but dropped out of college. She tried an x-ray program at Milwaukee but gave up on that, too. She finally was graduated in her mid-30s from the University of Wisconsin-Green Bay with a degree in geography.

Money from insurance and a settlement from the *Bluebelle* owner enabled her to travel across the United States, including a year in Colorado with a boyfriend. But she rarely settled down for long, and always returned to Green Bay.

She sometimes believes that she was seeking her father in those nomadic travels. She first married in 1971; a union that produced her first child, Brook. They divorced and she married again in 1976 and lived in West Berlin where her husband was stationed while serving in the army. From that marriage came children Blair and Brian.

Terry Jo is now Tere Fassbender and enjoys her three grandchildren.

Terry Jo has been Tere since she changed her name at the age of 16—"to give me a new identity." Today—45 years later—she is Tere Fassbender, married seven years to Ronald Fassbender, whom she met while both were working for the state Department of Natural Resources in water management at Oshkosh. They live in Kewaunee, a small Wisconsin town on Lake Michigan. Her three children are grown now, and between her and her husband at last count they had three grandchildren with another one due.

Richard Logan, a retired professor of human development at the University of Wisconsin-Green Bay who worked with her for several years in gathering material for a book about her, told me, "She's a remarkable woman. She's one of my heroes. With all of the tragedies in her life, she remains vibrant and energetic."

He describes her as something of a tomboy, with sun bleached hair; a person who smiles a lot, loves the outdoors and is good with animals.

As Tere Fassbender she appears to be at peace. She and her husband, both retired, are enjoying life, she says. They fish and hunt and dress up in historical re-enactments. She has been a fabric artist for many years, and her husband is involved in preserving the lakeshore. They love playing with their grandchildren.

"I don't think about that night very often any more," she said. "I'm over it."

And I don't think about Mary Jordan very often any more, either, but when I do she's always the young and playful Mary and I still wonder, what did she really mean when she placed that message in my typewriter a half century ago?

¤

30 • Is Anyone Listening?

They call it synergy today. A company owns a chain of newspapers, radio and television stations, a cable channel, a book publishing company and a few other communication-related businesses. It's no longer journalism; it's a provider of information. The units in the company share resources and use them in different venues.

But we didn't call it synergy when an announcer from WIRE, the radio station on the sixth floor, would race into the city room a few minutes before airtime to broadcast "the 6 o'clock news direct from the city room of *The Indianapolis Star.*" We were all slightly contemptuous of the young announcers; the same contempt we had for the fledgling television reporters.

The announcer would grab the carbons of news stories written by reporters for the first edition and race to a microphone in a corner of the newsroom. The announcer gave himself little or no time to assess what stories were worth broadcasting. Very often whatever was at the top of the pile of carbons became the lead item on the five-minute broadcast.

Driving home one evening I turned on the car radio to see what our man had to enlighten the public. The reader excitedly told us about a shoe store opening in the new Eagledale shopping center. His next item concerned a hardware store opening in the Eagledale shopping center. And so it went; one store after another opening its doors at the Eagledale shopping center.

He obviously had grabbed the carbons of stories written for a special advertising section to run later in the week.

That wasn't quite as embarrassing as the night the broadcaster told his listeners about the death of Hilton U. Brown, one of the city's leaders and onetime editor of *The Indianapolis News*. He rattled off the great man's achievements. But Mr. Brown was still with us. The announcer had picked up the carbons of a prepared obituary of Mr. Brown—one of more than a hundred such obits that were prepared of prominent citizens to be pulled from a file cabinet when they died.

There were no calls from Mr. Brown or from any listener telling us that the old gentleman was still with us. No complaints from the company brass, either.

In fact, even the station received no calls, the announcer admitted when he showed up at 5:55 p.m. the next day.

It confirmed what we had thought about the broadcasts. Nobody listened to them.

31 • A 63-Hour Ordeal

The city has produced its share of bizarre incidents that were staged to gain the attention of the media but none quite like the one carried out by Anthony Kiritsis over a three-day period in February 1977.

It began at 8 o'clock on a cold morning when Tony, then 44, walked into the downtown office of the real estate firm of Hall-Hottel Company, a firm affiliated with Meridian Mortgage Company, at 123 East Market Street. The companies were run by three Hall brothers—Dick, Bill and Jack.

When Dick Hall arrived at 8:10 a. m. Tony, who had business with the firm, asked him, "Have you got a minute?"

They went into Hall's office where Kiritsis telephoned 911 to report that he was holding Hall hostage. He then used a coat hanger as a noose around Hall's neck and attached it to a sawed-off shotgun with the muzzle pressed firmly against the back of Hall's neck. Kiritsis had his finger in a metal ring that was wired to the trigger. Kiritsis held Hall captive for the next 63 hours.

He walked his 42-year-old hostage down four flights of stairs. As they stepped out of the building, witnesses said they heard the short, stubby Kiritsis tell Hall, "Now I am going to take you out in the cold and blow your head off."

A police chaplain pleads with Kiritsis to free Dick Hall as they walk along Washington Street. Jim Young, a News *photographer, took the photo.*

As they emerged from the building, Jim Young, a photographer for *The News*, alerted to the abduction by a police radio at the paper, was already there. He said that Kiritsis at first led Hall to get to his car in a nearby garage, but it was the wrong garage. When they came out, Kiritsis changed plans and forced Hall to walk south on Pennsylvania Street to Washington Street where they headed west. Several policemen—and Young—trailed the pair as they walked by horrified onlookers. A police chaplain following them kept hollering, "Tony. Tony wait. Let's talk."

Young said he stopped following Kiritsis briefly when he realized that he had only one roll of film and two dollars. He stopped to telephone the city desk and said to send someone with film and a long lens. Then he popped into a photo shop, grabbed a handful of film, told the clerk to bill *The News*, and raced to catch up. Throughout the procession on the downtown streets, Young kept taking dramatic pictures. For a while he was the only photographer shooting; then others, including television cameramen, showed up.

Young said that Kiritsis and Hall once fell on the icy sidewalk. They got up and continued on to Senate Avenue where a police car had pulled crosswise in the middle of the intersection. The driver got out of the car and left the door open. Kiritsis turned to one of the policemen and told him to give him his revolver. He stuck the revolver in his back pocket, got into the driver's side of the police car and yanked Hall in after him. He ordered Hall to drive, Young said.

When a caravan of police cars followed them, Young said he and Chuck Robinson, an Associated Press photographer, induced a passing motorist to follow the procession. He gave them a perilous ride over icy Washington Street.

The procession ended at Crestwood Village West on Rockville Road where Kiritsis had an apartment. The 110 units in the building were evacuated because Kiritsis warned the police that he had wired the place with explosives. During the long siege some 500 of the residents in five of the other eight buildings in the complex also were evacuated. Young said he spent most of the next 60 hours camped out at the complex. Two elderly women residents in another building in the complex offered to let him and other photographers sleep in their apartments. He said they also cooked meals for them. Young stayed at the scene because, he said, "I wanted to be there when the cops stormed the place."

The pair settled in Kiritsis's third-floor apartment. He kept Hall a prisoner in his bathroom where he fed him. Negotiations began with Hall's brother, William Hall. Tony demanded that he be released from a 3-year-old $130,000 mortgage.

Kiritsis was using the loan to help develop 17 acres of land at Rockville Road and Lyndhurst Drive into a small shopping center. He was convinced that the mortgage company was working against him, hoping that he would be unable to develop his 17 acres and would default on the loan and they would pick up the land, which was then valued at $500,000. He seethed for months and made his move on that morning of February 8.

Westside residents remembered Tony as a young man driving an ice cream wagon up and down the streets in spring, summer and fall. His family made the ice cream. He was known to be a hard worker but was high strung and emotional.

He had four brothers and a sister. After their Greek immigrant parents died, Tony was chosen to manage the family's small mobile home park at 5333 West Vermont Street that his sister Effie had inherited. He lived in the park and worked hard and long hours running it. He had hoped to expand it. But when one of his brothers accused him of misusing funds generated by the park, Kiritsis's temper exploded. Police said he held Effie hostage with an axe until his brothers agreed to pay him $55,000, an amount he considered his due for his work at the park. With that money and the loan from Meridian Mortgage, Kiritsis set out to develop the center.

The standoff lasted two and a half days while Tony negotiated with the mortgage company, the cops and the prosecutor's office. He periodically called Fred Heckman, a local radio announcer. On the third day he announced that he would hold a "press conference" that evening, saying he wanted a nationwide television audience. By then nearly 100 reporters and photographers were camped out at the complex. We had six reporters and four photographers at the scene for the press conference.

Surrounded by helpless cops, Kiritsis marched into the lobby of the building with his prisoner. With the shotgun attached to Hall's neck, Kiritsis began yelling at reporters, "I'm a goddamned national hero and don't you forget it." He began his tirade at 10:15 p.m. His clothes were sweat-stained and he had a three-day growth of beard. He laced his rambling comments about the firm with profanities and obscenities. At times he would scream, yell, cry and then laugh. His harangue went on for 23 minutes.

At one point he ordered Hall to read a list of seven wrongs he said the firm had committed, but Hall was unable to talk because of the coat hanger wire squeezing his neck. So Kiritsis grabbed the list and read them himself.

Airing the tirade on live television was a concern for the TV stations. Lee Giles, WISH-TV news director, said announcer Mike Ahern telephoned him at home to ask whether they should stay with the broadcast. Giles said he had not been watching television. He said Kiritsis's language and the fear that he might blow Hall's brains out on live TV posed a dilemma for the stations. WISH decided to stay on the air but one of the stations signed off until it was over, Giles said.

"None of us had ever been involved in a thing like that," Giles said. "We felt like we were being used by Kiritsis. It really was a defining moment in how to handle a situation like that." Today with hand-held cameras available, Giles said the stations would position a reporter at the scene and describe what was going on, rather than letting the subject have free rein.

One of our reporters, Joe Gelarden, was in the room where Kiritsis was holding forth. Don Thrasher, another *Star* reporter, and Bud Berry, a *Star* photographer, also were in the room with other reporters, and cameramen from the television stations. Here's how Joe remembered that night 27 years later in a message he sent me:

> I will never forget the night he surrendered. We were in the apartment clubhouse. He came in and was surrounded by cops and TV camera crews.
>
> Thrasher and Bud Berry went to the front. I went to the back where there was a bank of phones. I called you. I had the only working phone. The guy from the *Chicago Tribune* wanted it—really wanted it. But I got [Lieutenant] Joe Ernst of the Sheriff's Department to keep him away. I started talking to you, thinking I was dictating. After about 10 minutes you said, 'This is the most dramatic thing I ever heard. Let me give you Len Castle [rewriteman].'
>
> We were convinced Tony was going to blow Dick Hall's head off....
>
> As Tony kept talking about alleged injustices and how he had been treated, filled with profanities that reminded me of my Marine Corps days, he got more and more intense, and began shouting. His raw language and the fear that Kiritsis would

> pull the trigger gave TV people fits.
>
> 'He is going to do it,' said Ernst.
>
> We were right on deadline. I yelled at Bud Berry to get his tail back to 307. 'but, but, but,' he said. I yelled at him that his photos were not worth a damn if we couldn't get them in the morning paper.
>
> Moments later, Tony backed off. Larry Broderick [sheriff] led him to a back room that had been set up as a command center. Their path went past me and as they turned a right corner, the shotgun pointed at me from about four feet away. Rather unsettling to say the least. Ernst and I just looked at each other and smiled.
>
> I went outside where the old Chevy staff car was parked, fired up the motor and got on the old 2-way radio. I couldn't reach you at first because Circulation was directing trucks to various locations. Then I heard a shot. I thought he had committed suicide. If he had shot Hall, the cops would have fired a thousand shots into his body.
>
> But no, Larry Broderick, who could talk a Democrat into voting for Richard Nixon, had talked him down and released Hall.
>
> Tony had walked outside with the weapon and fired the only round into the air.
>
> We really thought we were going to witness a blood bath. We thought Tony would shoot Hall and the cops would execute him and a bunch of spectators, read reporters and photogs.

Jim Young said that the wire around Hall's neck was so tight that Kiritsis could not free it. After he surrendered, police used wire clippers to free him. Tony had warned the police that the door to his apartment was wired with explosives, but after his surrender they checked the apartment and discovered two gallons of gasoline, but no explosives.

All of those promises of immunity during negotiations were hollow and Tony was jailed on charges of kidnapping, armed extortion and armed robbery. His performance triggered a rash of similar hostage-takings across the country.

During the months he was jailed he ranted that the police, the judges and prosecutors were all against him. He went to trial in October of that year. After three weeks a jury ruled that he was insane when he committed the crimes.

Kiritsis refused to be examined by a state-appointed psychiatrist, so he spent nearly three years in Larue Carter Hospital, a facility for mental patients. He periodically called us at the paper to complain about conditions at the hospital. He said the attendants were rude and sometimes drunk, that they gambled on the job and smuggled contraband to the patients.

He almost always found time to complain, too, that the press was mistreating him. Occasionally I'd get one of his calls. He would start out being polite and reasonable, but it wasn't long before the volume went up and the language went down.

Then it was time to say, "Nice talking to you, Tony." Click

After a decade in mental hospitals, he was released in January, 1988. His health was poor and he never really recovered. He was found dead in his Speedway home in the 1500 block of Mickley Avenue on January 28, 2005. The coroner's office said he died of natural causes.

Hall, too, was never the same after the three days as Kiritsis's prisoner, a relative confirmed. He's alive and retired but his brothers are deceased and their company is no longer in business.

¤

Photographer Jerry Clark displays the front page showing Kiritsis at his press conference just before he released Hall. Other staffers, including Bob Early (top right), gathered at a tavern near The Star *to unwind after putting out the final edition.*

32 • Posvar's Stories

Some of our better reporters in those early years had little or no college training. They learned on the job. And we hired a few job hoppers (mostly copy editors) who drifted from city to city. They worked a few weeks or months and then moved on. Many were alcoholics. Some of those hired were back for a second chance. They had once been staff members before alcohol or the breakup of a marriage had ended their stays at *The Star.*

A few returned months or years later for one last chance after convincing Early that they had reformed and were eager to work. We'd see them for a couple of weeks until they picked up their paychecks on Wednesday, and they'd be gone. A few stayed on, remained sober, and became productive members of the staff.

One of the more notable characters on the staff was Vladimir Lester Posvar. He had worked on a dozen newspapers before joining *The Star* late in life. "Pos" had also served in the Army for a number of years, retiring as a colonel. While he enjoyed a few beers, Pos was no alcoholic.

In the 1930s he was working on the old *Cleveland News* as its sole editorial writer. His job was to fill the daily editorial page with as much interesting material as he could round up from the wire services and the newspaper syndicates, and also to write the local editorials. He found himself running dry of ideas for a lead editorial on the day that Eleanor Roosevelt was to visit Cleveland, so he composed an editorial that noted that the while the *News* was a Republican paper and had often disagreed with her husband, "We think it fitting that she receive a 21-gun salute the same as her husband." So the next 21 lines read "boom…boom…boom" And because of a spacing problem, Posvar put the headline in 24-point type and he reduced the size of the type gradually down to agate.

Posvar said Mrs. Roosevelt said she liked the editorial, but the newspaper executives didn't appreciate it and they fired him. Pos insisted the real reason he got sacked was that he was earning $65 a week during the Depression while new graduates of journalism schools were willing to work for $15 a week. The paper later rehired him, he said.

Pos sometimes spent his lunch hour in nearby bars. After a couple of beers, he reverted to his military ways—straightening his shoulders, clicking his heels and addressing co-workers in formal, military style. One of the security guards found himself pinned against the wall in the building's main entrance one afternoon. Posvar had his finger in the guard's chest, telling the fellow, "You're a disgrace to your uniform."

The guard took the dressing down without complaint but Pos wasn't so fortunate when a policeman warned him about jaywalking near Meridian and Ohio streets. It was a hot summer day and the policeman was perspiring heavily. His short-sleeved shirt was soaked and untucked. One of the copy editors wives working in the drugstore at the intersection saw Posvar assume his military bearing and inform the cop, "You're out of uniform."

That was enough to get him arrested for public intoxication. He was shoved in a paddy wagon and taken to the lockup. About an hour later Charley Griffo, an assistant managing editor, got a call from a policeman in the lockup, who asked, "You got a guy named Posvar over there?"

"Yeah," Griffo said.

"Then come and get him. He's holding close-order drill in the drunk tank."

Posvar had entertained us with tales of his many experiences in the military and on other newspapers. I suggested to him in 1970 that he write down some of the stories.

He surprised me a few days later when he handed me a list of 22 articles that he said he planned to write. Over the next few months he would give me one of the articles. They were interesting but I didn't know what to do with them. I always felt guilty that I hadn't done something with them. So after he died, I gave them to the Indiana Historical Society where they are available today.

The stories related that he was born the son of Czech immigrants in Butler County, Kansas, in 1902. He left home at 15 and enlisted in the army during World War I when he was 16. He said he lied to the enlistment officer that he was 18.

He said he worked on 11 newspapers, beginning with *The Topeka Daily Capital* on March 19, 1919 while attending Washburn University in Topeka where he graduated at the top of his class. Before joining *The Star*, he had worked on papers in Kansas City, Topeka, Cleveland, Cincinnati, Detroit, and even worked two weeks on the *New York World* in 1929. He came to *The Star* from the *Indianapolis Times* after it folded in 1965, and then wound up his career on the copy desk of *The Indianapolis News*.

In the early 1930s working on the *Cleveland News* he was sent out to determine if it was true that a prominent Englishman's son was engaged to a local girl. When the father arrived in Cleveland, Pos buttonholed him to ask whether his son was indeed engaged to the girl. He wouldn't answer so Pos said he kept asking. Finally, Pos said the man "shook his cane at me, and growled, 'Only a cad would ask such a question.'"

It was Winston Churchill, then Britain's Chancellor of the Exchequer.

Among the memoirs he left with me were tales of exploits he experienced during World War II. He was particularly proud of capturing 24 naked Germans. He was on the island of Pantelleria that sits between Tunisia and Sicily. The Allies had just captured the island. The Germans had been aboard a mail boat that arrived from Naples. Unaware that the Allies had captured the island, the crewmen decided to have a swim after docking the boat. Each of them put their clothes on the dock and dove into the water. About then Pos and another officer came across them and ordered them to surrender, which they did.

During the war Posvar served as an Army captain, and was awarded the Silver Star for heroism in battle in Italy.

I got a lot of mileage retelling this story Pos told about a *New York Daily News* copy editor who wrote a prize-winning headline on a story about a wedding. The story concerned a bride whose white gown was so snug that she went into labor at the altar and was rushed to the hospital where she delivered her baby. The headline, "Baby Gives Bride Away," took up the front page of the tabloid. The *Daily News* regularly awarded $25 to the editor writing the best headline each week, but this time, Posvar said, the publisher, Capt. Bob Patterson, declared, "It's the best in 10 weeks. Pay him $250."

In another of his articles Pos said he was working for the Associated Press in Santo Domingo in the Dominican Republic when Rafael Trujillo y Molina came to power. Pos wrote an article pointing out that gangsters from the United States had put Trujillo in power by rigging the election. As a result, one of Trujillo's aides challenged him to a duel. When the aide discovered that Posvar was a crack shot, he backed off. But Pos was jailed for writing the article and then deported. He later returned and even became an aide and advisor to Trujillo.

His son Wesley also had an illustrious military—and academic—career. Born in 1929, he was graduated from West Point in 1946 with the highest academic standing in the class. He entered the Air Force before it was severed from the Army. He became a pilot and retired in 1967 also with the rank of colonel. He flew 27 bombing missions in Vietnam. His last assignment was at the Air Force Academy as a professor. After retiring from the Air Force, he joined the faculty at West Point, and later became the chancellor of the University of Pittsburgh.

His years in the military had toughened Pos. When the city was shut down by a blizzard in 1978, few citizens were able to step outside during the four days that the city was locked down. But not Pos. On the morning after the blizzard hit on January 26, he showed up at work at *The News*. He had hitchhiked from his home 12 miles away. He was 76 years old.

Later that day after working a full shift on the copy desk, he stopped at a tavern a half block from the paper. The next day the concerned tavern owner called the city desk to ask if Posvar had made it home. He said Pos had bought a six-pack of beer and announced that he was walking home. To make certain that he had arrived home safely, someone from *The News* called his home to inquire if he made it. Pos said he was puzzled why anyone would doubt his ability to find his way home.

He continued to work until he was 86.

Telling Posvar's story finally has eased my guilt.

¤

33 • Open House at The Star

Until the papers became security conscious and grilled visitors at the front entrance before allowing them access to the building, the newsrooms were magnets for poets and drunks, saints and sinners, the lonely and oppressed, ex-convicts, mothers of runaway daughters, battered wives, and husbands angry about outrageous support payments.

There were a lot of drifters who made their way from city to city, dragging along dog-eared clippings to prove that editors elsewhere had considered their exploits worth noting in the local papers. They were crossing the country on roller skates, bicycles, horses, or in wagons or vintage cars. The cross-country walkers always mentioned the number of pairs of shoes they had worn out. A few mendicants claimed to be raising money for a cause, but most of the visitors simply wanted their jaunts recorded in the paper. And they relied on what they believed to be a sure-fire gimmick for photo coverage—diverting their trip around the 2.5-mile track at the Indianapolis Motor Speedway.

Proponents of startling religious cults showed up with rigid smiles and fervid determination. They were tougher to discourage than the cross-country trekkers.

At election time, candidates, or their public relations minions, showed up seeking press coverage. It was usually the perennial losers who felt they weren't getting a fair shake from the political party. One of the most persistent was a squat, swarthy retired merchant seaman named E. J. Rocker. After several unsuccessful runs for office, Rocker decided that he needed to get his name mentioned first on the ballot, so he changed it to Aocker.

In a guest column that he wrote for *The News* in 1974, E. J. said he had run for office 17 times, twice for mayor, "maybe four or five times for Congress," and several municipal offices, all without success. When he ran for Congress the first time in 1944, he said, "I drove a horse and buggy downtown to campaign."

In a 1972 interview with *Star* columnist Tom Keating he told why he had fared so poorly in his quests for office. Aocker laid the blame on the Republican Party for refusing to indorse him. "One thing bugs me," he told Keating. "A lot of the candidates like Humphrey and Wallace are using ideas I've been putting out for years on things like tax relief and cutting foreign aid. They've all been copying me this year."

One night William Erbecker, a police court lawyer running once again for some office, probably prosecutor, came to the city room trying to induce a political writer to give him a story to bolster a campaign that was going nowhere. His plea went unanswered so he thought he would pick up a few votes while he was in the building. He went through the halls dropping his campaign cards on his way out.

Booze was Erbecker's problem and not only with the press and the party. On an airplane trip to Miami he tried to impress a stewardess by confiding, "I'm a professional killer." He was hauled off the plane at Louisville.

Another visitor, a state legislator and farmer who looked like a cross between Abraham Lincoln and a scarecrow, had been the subject of some amusing stories in the paper. One afternoon he entered the city room pushing a wheelbarrow loaded with tomatoes, muskmelon, squash and other fresh vegetables. "Here, catch," he yelled, and then threw vegetables to almost everyone in the room. At first the reporters thought he was angry at the paper for making fun of him, but he was polite and the staff thanked him for the vegetables.

And then there was the call from the Reverend Charles Colton, another perennial luckless political aspirant. He wanted the paper to publish an obituary announcing his funeral service before he died. He said he planned to preach at the service and deliver his own eulogy. His reasoning? He said he wanted friends and would-be mourners to be able to talk to him instead of gazing at him in a casket.

A portly woman in a gaudy dress—one of several marginal candidates running for the Presidency that year—employed an unusual campaign technique. She raced around the city room kissing everyone who couldn't escape, and offered each a drink from a bottle of whiskey.

She was not the only kissing visitor. Apparently carried away with the spirit of Christmas one year, beefy Bess Watson, the legendary obituary writer for *The News*, tried to kiss everyone who couldn't get out of her way. Allen Jeffries, a broadcaster for Radio Station WIRE, was in the city room and wasn't quick enough to avoid Bess's busses. "Now I know what it feels like to get knocked down and run over by a sprinkler truck," he commented.

If the supplicants for coverage didn't come to the city room, they were on the telephone with their requests. One gent named Curt called to ask that we take a picture of the first birthday of his Irish setter. He was inviting in other Irish setters to celebrate on St. Patrick's Day. We might have sent a photographer if Curt could have lined up the setters at the table for ice cream and cake.

Two days before Easter we heard from a woman who thought we'd like to take a photo of her boyfriend and his father because both had identical tattoos of rabbits on their chests.

Job applicants often came up with gimmicks but few could outdo the appeal from a woman in Oklahoma who wrote on flowered stationery:

> I am publishing now a sizable number of deep, rapturous classics of romance, intrigue, sophisticated unreality. They are startling in mystery and relative to the fine arts.
>
> I can come to Indianapolis for an interview or appointment and would consider a change of address or assignment overseas.
>
> I am a beauty, a mezzo soprano, and I drink and I like involvement.
>
> I have lived in Havana, Paris, and Berlin.

An intriguing resume but we passed on her anyway.

Nor could we help the woman who addressed her plea to the "News Media c/o Public Relations" that somehow ended up on my desk. She wrote:

> Help! Help! Help!
>
> I am an Evangelist Missionary and I am in trouble.
>
> I need the voice of this press to speak to the good citizens of Indianapolis will you help me?
>
> I am a lone woman. A mother and grandmother of three small school children we are called the Five Missionaries. I am fighting for recognition. It is imperative. A matter of life or death.
>
> Will you please help me?

A young boy named Brad Bates had a novel approach for attention. His typewritten letter, dated December 9, 1974, stated, "I have an article for the *Star*." On a separate sheet his one-sentence article declared: "Jeffrey Bates of 6364 Brookline Drive is probably the only eleven-year-old boy in the city who does needlepoint while sitting on the toilet."

The city room was not the only place in the building that attracted unusual visitors. One morning a young man showed up at the Want-Ad counter just off the front entrance. He was greeted by an eager 18-year-old clerk on her first day on the job.

He came through the door carrying a cat and an empty Lavoris bottle. Somewhat dismayed, the clerk looked him over and then asked, "May I help you?"

"Yes you can," he said. "I've just killed my family with this mouthwash bottle and I want to place an ad in the paper so everyone will know."

This was not the sort of want-ad she expected, so she asked the young man to wait while she sought her boss, Paul Schultz, the classified advertising manager.

Schultz, almost as dismayed as the clerk, gingerly tried to engage the man in conversation, getting nowhere. So he asked, "Would you like to go to the bathroom?"

The man looked puzzled but said, "Well, I guess so."

Paul quickly ushered the man out the front door.

But a few seconds later, he barged back into the room, threw the cat on the floor, whacked it with the bottle and smashed the bottle against the wall. It shattered. Then he took off all of his clothes and began jumping in the glass with his bare feet.

The young clerk dove under the counter. Schulz called for a security guard, who said he couldn't help because he had to make his rounds in the building. So Paul grabbed the man and threw a coat around him. Finally the police arrived to subdue him.

A few minutes later, the clerk grabbed her purse and left the building. She never returned.

¤

34 • An In-House Joke Backfires

Each summer ECP hosted a Sunday picnic for all of the employees and their families at the Fourth Estate, the recreation area he established soon after buying the papers.

The skeleton staff working in the newsroom on those Sundays missed the picnic but could count on the promotion director, Fred Howenstine, to bring a basket of food to the city room. Through a mix-up or oversight, the food never arrived.

So Jep Cadou, Jr., who was assigned to write the puff piece about the picnic for the Monday paper, decided to have a little fun at Howenstine's expense. He started each paragraph with the letters of Howenstine's name. He began "Hundreds of (blah, blah) and started the next paragraph with an "O." And on it went until the first letter of each paragraph spelled "HOWENSTINE EATS IT."

The staff chuckled at the inside joke but Joe Shepard, one of the more militant members of the Newspaper Guild (the staff's bargaining unit), thought he could aid the guild's cause by letting management know that the joke was just one more indication of low morale of the staff. When he learned about the story, Early exploded. He called a meeting of the entire staff (bringing in even those on their days off). He climbed on top of a desk in the city room and ranted about the evils of anyone using the pages of *The Indianapolis Star* for such levity.

After the chastisement, Jep said he went to Early's office and told him, "I'm going to quit."

"Now just wait a minute, Jep," Early told Cadou and then talked him out of leaving.

In one of his more perplexing decisions a few weeks later Early promoted Jep to sports editor, an appointment that didn't sit well with the sports staff and, in fact, turned out to be a major blunder. Shepard, who had no part in the hoax except to use it as a bargaining tool, didn't fare so well. Early assigned him to work the night shift at police headquarters.

Early and Shepard had a strained relationship for years. Joe had been one of the paper's better reporters at one time but he was outspoken and independent and had an affinity for alcohol.

Helen Connor recalled that one night while working on the copy desk she heard Early, then city editor, and Shepard get into a shouting match over some story. She said that Early yelled across the room, "I ought to punch you in the nose." That brought Shepard out of his chair. He trotted to the city desk and said, "Here I am." Early looked up and said, "Oh, go sit down."

The Howenstine affair was not the only instance when The Star's pages became the target of levity.

An Indianapolis physician called the women's department to report about his British guests for the 500-Mile Race. Donna Mullinix, who was running the desk that week in the editor's absence, said the man was careful to say the couple was royalty from Liverpool, so knowing the department needed a picture for its pages, she assigned a photographer to get a shot of the couple. The photographer noted that their name was given as Sir and Lady Ossis of Liverpool. An editor on the copy desk wrote the lines for the picture and it ran in the first edition. Someone on the desk recognized Sir Ossis of Liverpool as a local actor, so the photo was killed after the first edition.

Donna said Bob Early was so furious when he heard about it that he ordered that the family's name never be mentioned in the paper again. She said that when the doctor's daughter was getting engaged, he had to beg Early to relent and run her picture and the announcement.

"Needless to say, I was the laughing stock of the editorial department," Donna said.

Reporters enjoy misleading reporters working against them.

Before I was hired, Shepard had covered a murder trial in southern Indiana. It was labeled the "hands and feet" murder because the killer had hacked off the victim's hands and feet, as well as his head.

During a break in the trial Joe was eating lunch at the local Elks Club with a deputy prosecutor. He spoke in confidential tones but loud enough for a reporter sitting at an adjacent table to hear the conversation.

"You really going to enter them into evidence?" Joe asked the prosecutor, who was a party to the ruse.

"Yeah, tomorrow," the deputy replied.

"Where've they been?"

"In cold storage."

With that the other reporter left the table and phoned his paper to say that the amputated hands and feet were to be entered into evidence. And the paper went with the story.

While such subterfuge might have pleased Early because it affected another paper, he was adamant that no jokes of any kind should ever get in the pages of *The Star*. Don't even think about planting an April Fool's Day joke in the paper.

Seven months before I began at the paper a three-year-old girl in San Marino, California, was playing in an overgrown field when she fell 90 feet through a 14-inch-wide abandoned well. Her name was Kathy Fiscus. Rescuers attempted to rescue her by digging a parallel shaft. For several days it was front page news across the country. Among the volunteers who showed up to help were tiny people offering to be lowered into the pipe to rescue the little girl.

Someone on the news desk had the idea of graphically showing the size of the well opening by overlaying a thin circle 14 inches in diameter over the front page. A brilliant idea to the *Star* staffers, but not to the publisher. Pulliam called it a grandstand move and issued instructions that no such tampering be allowed in his papers.

The workers finally succeeded in reaching Kathy after 50 hours but it was too late. The little girl was dead.

¤

35 • A Fearless Reporter

Carolyn Pickering Lautner was the kind of reporter that every newspaper would like to have but seldom find. She was bright, educated, fearless and dogged when pursuing a story. She regularly won journalism awards —local, state and national. And in off hours she raised two children and won golf tourneys. Her ability to ask tough questions without being abrasive was one of her talents. Another was knowing when to listen.

Carolyn Pickering

She was hired during World War II when she was a student at Butler University where she edited the college newspaper, the *Butler Collegian*. At *The Star* she covered the police beat as a cub reporter, an uncommon job for a woman in those years. After graduating from Butler, she received a grant to attend Columbia University but left after one semester, contending that she had learned more about journalism at *The Star* than what she was getting in the classroom. She took a job with the *Herald-American* in Chicago, got married and had two children. When her marriage to an older man, a classical musician, didn't work out, she called Bob Early and he invited her to come back to *The Star*. That would have been about 1952. She remained with the paper until 1978 when she lost her enthusiasm for reporting. She then became a successful real estate agent.

She covered the Federal beat for many years, reporting on trials, bankruptcies, and raids by the FBI and Federal marshals. She didn't always please the officials and Federal judges she covered, but they conceded that she was fair and honest.

She showed some of her fearlessness on a February afternoon in 1954 when an escaped mental patient showed up in the city room. He approached her desk and demanded to talk to the city editor. She sensed that he was the man who had been calling her to complain about conditions at Central State Hospital where he had been confined. She became wary of the way he held a hand in his pocket. She conversed with him and learned that he had twice escaped from Central State, the last time 10 months earlier. He rambled on about torture practiced there. "Pick" became the sympathetic listener and got him to agree to come back later that day when she said she would have more time to interview him.

After he left, she checked on him and learned that he was a dangerous psychopath with a persecution complex, and that he was being sought for trying to kill two men on a train. The staff in the newsroom was alerted and several policemen were called in to await his return. The cops were stationed in the adjoining mailroom corridor. When the man walked in he sensed that something was amiss and he began cursing, and turned to leave but two reporters, Ed Cotton and Rick Johnson, tackled him and the cops rushed in to handcuff him.

The incident earned her a Pall Mall award that carried a $500 prize. It was also dramatized on a television show sponsored by Pall Mall cigarettes.

Pick was nearly gunned down by another ex-Central State patient four months later. She was in the office one morning when she heard on the police radio about a policeman being shot by a man barricaded in a west-side home. She rushed to the scene and discovered that a mental patient had holed up in his house and was staging a standoff with police. In what became known as the Battle of Elder Avenue, the crazed gunman fired bullets at the police from 11:30 a. m. until 1:30 p. m.

The standoff began after the gunman, Howard Ellis, ordered his wife, Janie Ellis, and five children out of the house. His wife told the police that he was threatening to shoot her. They were living in the house at 733 North Elder Avenue along with the five children placed there by the Marion County Welfare Department.

The shootout began when Patrolmen Chris Greenwood and Robert Yates approached the house to investigate the complaint of a domestic disturbance—one of those assignments police dread because they never know how the subjects will react. In this case, Ellis opened fire and shot both of them. During the next two hours, Ellis shot nine other policemen, wounding eight of them seriously. Ellis withstood machine gun fire from two armored cars and tear gas tossed into the splintered house. By the time the standoff ended more than 250 city and state police and sheriff's deputies had been at the scene.

It ended after the police fired at three sides of the house while four policemen rushed inside the house where they fatally shot Ellis.

Pick was one of several reporters at the scene. She said she was crouched behind a small tree some 100 yards from the house when Buford Cadle, a member of the State Police Board, blared through a bullhorn, "It's OK. We got him." She said she straightened up and a bullet whizzed over her head.

She showed her versatility when she was assigned to guard and care for a two-headed baby just a few months before Howard Ellis took a shot at her on Elder Avenue.

The baby was born on December 12, 1953 in the Daviess County Hospital and was transported to James Whitcomb Riley Hospital in Indianapolis where it remained three weeks.

The parents, Cecil and Margaret Hartley, lived with their three blonde-haired daughters ages 5, 4 and 2 in a tar-papered, four-room farmhouse in a remote part of Daviess County in southern Indiana. A coal stove in the kitchen and a coal grate in a bedroom heated the shack. Kerosene lamps lighted the cabin and their water came from an outdoor pump. To get to the cabin, vehicles had to plow through a road that became impassable in winter, or it could be reached on foot through a woodland path.

The twins, Daniel Kaye and Donald Ray, were joined at the waist but had two shoulders and four arms. The press was doing a job of exploiting the pathetic baby. And when the baby was due to be released from the hospital, an excited Charley Griffo, one of *The Star's* editors, arranged for Pick to accompany the baby and parents in an ambulance taking them back to their home. And, oh yes, she was told to stay down there and care for the babies but keep them hidden from reporters and photographers from other papers, principally *The News* and the *Times.*

She spent three days in the cabin, sleeping on a chair when she could. The three little girls slept on a cot.

"When we arrived, I called the pharmacist out of bed at 2 in the morning," she said. "We needed all sorts of things and the pharmacist was helpful." She said he opened the store and got her a supply of diapers, a huge kettle to wash them in and to sterilize the baby's bottles

"I didn't know what I was doing," she said even though she had two children of her own, 5 and 3. "One time one baby would be crying, and the other was asleep, and then it would wake up and the other one would go to sleep."

While trying to care for them, Pick said she barred other reporters and editors from getting into the cabin. She got some help from Jim Ramsey, a *Star* photographer who had driven to the house while Pick rode in the ambulance.

Pick said the father spent most of his time trying to wrangle a deal for the baby to be displayed in a carnival freak show.

She came home on the third day worn out but wrote a story about her experience.

"All that time I spent there and the paper wouldn't give me any overtime pay," Carolyn remembered years later.

The baby's condition worsened and it was returned to the hospital. It lived only three months.

I remember there was some discussion about whether we should publish a photo of the baby. As I remember, we did. Couldn't let the other papers scoop us on that, could we?

Pick was not easily intimidated. She withstood threats and pressure during many of her investigations. The pressure was never more intense than when she exposed the Reverend Jim Jones as a charlatan six years before he and his 900 followers committed mass suicide in a jungle retreat in Guyana in South America.

Jones, a charismatic preacher, was born in 1931 in the small farming community of Lynn, Indiana on the Ohio border. Its principal industry was manufacturing caskets. Jones's father, a member of the local Ku Klux Klan, was gassed in World War I and was unable to work. He died when Jones was an adolescent. Even then Jim Jones was described as strong and resilient with an explosive temper, but he showed a strong concern for the poor and downtrodden.

When he moved to Indianapolis he sold monkeys door to door, and between 1949 and 1964 he built up a ministry attracting a preponderance of poor African-Americans. They met in the People's Temple at 975 North Delaware Street. His ministry appeared legitimate enough that the Disciples of Christ Church ordained him, though he lacked formal theological training.

Charles H. Boswell, who was mayor at the time, recalled that the city's Human Rights Commission had been having difficulty finding a director, but after Jones had been successful in integrating several of the restaurants in downtown Indianapolis, they felt that he was the ideal person for the job. "He did a good job," Boswell said.

Jones made a good appearance and he spoke well, Boswell said. He usually was seen on the street wearing turtlenecks and dark glasses. In the early 1960s he began adopting children to form an interracial family.

As concerns about his bizarre ministry intensified here, he moved his operation to California and settled in an area some seven miles from Ukiah, the seat of Mendocino County, 150 miles north of San Francisco. He took with him about 145 of his devoted followers. That was in 1965.

By 1972 Jones claimed the number of followers had increased to 4,000, but he was beginning to show signs of the messiah complex that would be his undoing. He was said to have raised 40 people from the dead, made the blind see and the cripple walk. Church members were calling him the Prophet of God.

Pick recognized that Jones and his followers were skidding toward disaster. She said she decided to investigate Jones after the paper got complaints from a Westside woman about her two daughters being lured to Jones's complex and being held virtual prisoners. While she began investigating, she was told that the Reverend Lester Kinsolving, a reporter for the *San Francisco Examiner*, was also investigating Jones and his church.

Jim Jones sold monkeys in Indianapolis when he was beginning his ministry around 1950.

They then collaborated on a two-month investigation.

She discovered records that showed that Jones had been involved in numerous property transactions here that involved real estate transfers which wound up in his name or that of a profit-making corporation controlled by Jones, his wife and his mother.

She interviewed ex-church members who accused Jones of "mass hypnosis," phony faith-healing practices and creating terror among those who dared to leave the church.

One of his followers who had returned to Indianapolis told Pick, "When we left Indianapolis, everyone in the group turned over whatever they had —money, property, furniture—to Jim Jones."

In California, 11 former Greyhound buses brought followers from as far as Seattle and Los Angeles to attend his four and five-hour services and his preaching to a background of rock music.

But there were increasing reports of beatings and torture of followers who did not conform to the church's demands. The People's Temple in the settlement near Ukiah was guarded by a minimum of four guards carrying side arms.

After the *Examiner* began publishing Kinsolving's reports, some 150 pickets picketed outside the *Examiner* building for nine hours. So effective was the pressure Jones put on the *Examiner* that the paper cancelled the last four articles of Kinsolving's eight-part series.

We began receiving official looking letters supporting Jones and accusing Pick of dishonest reporting. We ignored them. But pressure from the government caused the publisher, Gene Pulliam, to order that we stop publishing the stories after four of her six stories had run. Pick said she was told that the paper was violating Jones's right to religious freedom.

Whenever Jones felt threatened, he moved. He made several trips to Guyana in the late 1960s. In 1974 he took 50 church members to the hot and humid jungle clearing and by the end of 1977 most of his followers had left for Guyana to a socialist settlement now named Jonestown. As the years went on he formed liaisons with younger women in his burgeoning cult and bragged about his sexual prowess; that he could perform several times a day with either men or women. And he was telling his followers to throw away their Bibles; that he had the answers.

Within a year reports of beatings, secret gun caches and suicide drills in Jonestown became so intense that a California congressman, Leo J. Ryan, led a delegation to Jonestown on November 14, 1978, to investigate the reports. The group included Ryan's aides, Jones's lawyer, members of the press and family members concerned about the treatment of their children at the settlement.

At the settlement Ryan talked to Jones and interviewed some of the people, including a dozen or more who asked his help in escaping. At the end of four days, they returned to the airfield to fly home. As they prepared to board the plane, Ryan and four members of his party were fatally shot. Five others were seriously wounded. That afternoon the charismatic Jones instructed his followers—men, women and children—to drink cyanide-laced Kool-Aid because he realized that Jonestown was doomed. One by one they followed his orders and at day's end more than 900 corpses, including Jones and his wife and their children, covered the grounds of Jonestown.

We never heard from any of the Jones defenders again.

¤

36 • Manson Was A Hoosier

The Reverend Jim Jones was not the only "messiah" with Indiana roots. The infamous Charles Manson, who with his followers, killed more than three dozen persons, spent most of his childhood in the state, and most of it behind bars.

Manson convinced his followers—young men and women from middle-class backgrounds—that their victims were symbols of corrupt society so it was their duty to kill them.

So convincing was the savvy leader that his followers thought of him as Christ returned. That claim prompted Griffo to suggest a bogus headline—"Jesus Was A Hoosier."

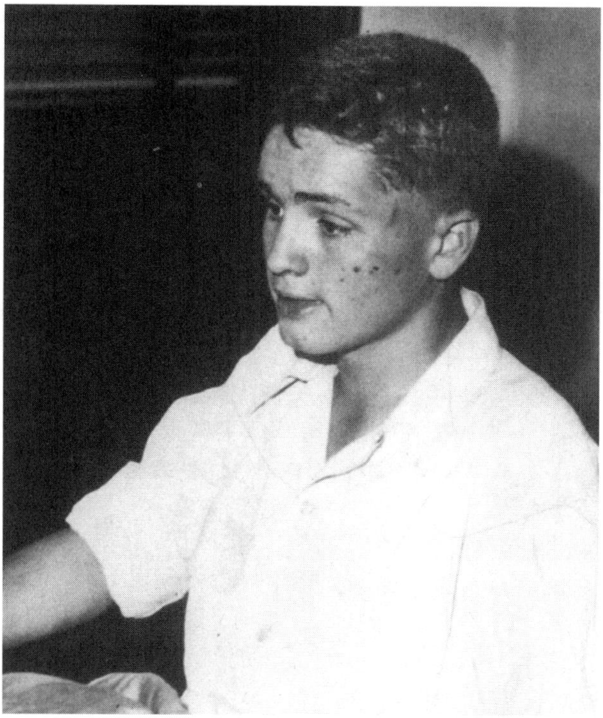

Charles Manson had a troubled life growing up in Indianapolis.

Manson had a tragic background. He was born in 1934 to a 16-year-old girl whom he later described as a "teen-age whore." After spending five years in prison for robbery, his mother reclaimed Manson, then eight years old, and they lived in a series of rundown motels.

When he was 12 he was sent to the Gibault School for Boys at Terre Haute. He spent 10 months there before running away. His mother didn't want him, so he ran away again. He began a long series of burglaries and thefts. He was put in the Marion County Juvenile Center but escaped the next day.

Authorities were erroneously informed that Manson was a Catholic, so arrangements were made for him to be sent to Father Flanagan's Boys Town. Four days after arriving he and another boy stole a car and drove to his uncle's home in Peoria, Illinois.

At 13 he was sent to the Boys School at Plainfield. He was there three years and ran away 18 times. In 1951 he fled to California. After being caught burglarizing, he was sent to the National Training School for Boys in Washington, D. C.

By the time he formed his family of followers in the Haight-Asbury section of San Francisco in 1967 Manson had spent 17 of his 32 years in institutions.

He became a mesmerizing figure, attracting hippie types infected with the radicalism of the sixties. He was older and smarter than his followers, and he was articulate, as well.

Convinced by Manson that society was sick, he and his followers murdered nine people between July 27 and August 26 in 1969. Five of the victims were slaughtered in the home of Hollywood film director Roman Polanski. They included Polanski's wife, actress Sharon Tate, who was eight months pregnant; an heiress to a coffee fortune and her jet set playboy paramour; an internationally known hair stylist, and a young man driving toward the gate to the estate just as the killers arrived. He was their first victim.

Manson bragged of committing 35 murders. He and some of the eight members of Manson's "family" are still in prison.

¤

37 • Millions For The Taking

Carolyn Pickering got her first impression of Marjorie Jackson in a Federal courtroom in the spring of 1976.

"She looked like a witch," Pick recalled. "They said she was a recluse and she looked like one." She was 66 years old and lived by herself in a spacious house on six acres on Spring Mill Road across from the Meridian Hills Country Club golf course.

She and Pickering were in a courtroom at the trial of Herbert Biddle Jr.; Pick as *The Star*'s reporter covering the trial, Marjorie Jackson as the victim of Biddle's embezzlement.

The chain of events that led to the death of Marjorie Jackson began in January that year when she noticed that someone had been stealing from her account at Indiana National Bank, the state's largest. Her account was invested principally in municipal bonds and she knew what sort of interest to expect. When the amount shrunk, she suspected that someone was stealing from the account. She was right. The banker in charge of her account was Biddle. Four months later Biddle was convicted of embezzling $700,000 from the account. He was sentenced to 10 years in Federal prison, later reduced to three years.

As soon as she suspected the embezzlement, Marjorie Jackson wanted nothing more to do with banks. She began withdrawing her money. She began by taking out $500,000 in stacks of new $100, $50 and $20 bills. She put the money in an old suitcase and transported it to her home in one of her two 1976-model Cadillacs (one for use in winter, one for summer). She continued to withdraw her funds over the next five months before closing the account. She had taken $9 million from the bank and stashed it throughout her house. Before turning over the money to her, the bank registered the serial numbers of the bills.

Removing her money was a fatal mistake. The bankers tried to talk her out of secreting the money in her home, as did law enforcement officials, but she rejected their advice. The bank even petitioned Marion Probate Court to give the bank guardian rights over her property, but Probate Judge Victor S. Pfau decided she was capable of handling her own funds; that she appeared mentally competent. She convinced Pfau that she would be depositing the money in other banks around the country.

She lived as a recluse in her home in the upscale neighborhood. A chain link fence overgrown with weeds guarded the grounds. When neighbors complained about the unsightly grounds, she told them that the Bible told her to leave them untended for seven years. She also made it clear that she disliked Catholics, Jews and blacks, and the neighborhood was heavily Jewish.

It wasn't long before word spread that she had millions of dollars in her home. Less than a month after she closed her account, a man broke into her attached garage, crept through a crawl space in the ceiling and entered her house. He opened the front door to let an accomplice enter. They left with a suitcase taken from the hall closet. It contained $817,000.

The pair lived lavishly on their loot and talked about the woman and her money. One of the men went on a three-month spree in Florida and Mexico City. The other one was beaten in his apartment by thugs wearing ski masks who took $200,000 from him. A third member of the group, a lookout, got skittish and talked to his minister about the crime. The minister reported it to the Marion County Prosecutor. Investigators put together a convincing case against the trio, but they needed her testimony about the burglary to prosecute the thieves. She refused, saying, "It must have been God's will."

When law enforcement officers went to her house to suggest that they provide surveillance, she refused and ordered them to leave. The county prosecutor, James F. Kelley, said he believed that she and her husband had been "skimming" their earnings for years and secreting the funds in her house. She was afraid of a tax audit, he surmised.

Marjorie had married Chester H. Jackson in 1952, but they had been together since the 1940s when Chester (long estranged from his wife) and his paternal grandfather became boarders at a neat, attractive home that Marjorie and her mother maintained in Woodruff Place, a neighborhood a few blocks east of Monument Circle. Woodruff Place had been the setting for Booth Tarkington's Pulitzer Prize-winning novel, *The Magnificent Ambersons*. The Jacksons had no children.

Chester's father owned a chain of grocery stores. Chester was in the chain's main store in downtown Indianapolis on May 27, 1931, when two bandits entered the store and fatally shot his father. Chester's testimony helped send both men to the electric chair. Chester inherited the stores, and his father's one-quarter ownership of Southwestern Illinois Coal Company. When the coal company was sold in 1972 (two years after Chester had died), Marjorie inherited one fourth of the proceeds. After taxes and legal fees, Marjorie was able to bank $9 million.

She and Chester had traveled extensively. One of their stops was at a

Moslem orphanage on a visit to the Holy Land. It changed the pattern of her life. She began spending Saturdays in her bedroom, observing the Sabbath and conversing with the Lord. In time she began observing a six-day Sabbath, communing with her God and often spending the night playing religious and classical music at one of the three pianos in her house. She had taken piano lessons from top pianists all over the world while traveling with her husband.

As word spread about the money in her house, the vultures descended. Law enforcement authorities had no idea how many times she might have been victimized.

One of those vultures was Howard R. Willard, a 38-year-old bully, a loudmouth and heavy drinker who lived in Mooresville a few miles southwest of Indianapolis. He lived with Marjorie S. Pollitt, who was 10 years his senior. They fought regularly and had been married twice and divorced twice. Willard had a lengthy police record, mainly for petty thefts.

The pair visited the Jackson home in January of 1977 and broke a gate to enter the grounds but failed to get inside the house. So Willard began looking for an accomplice, and after four months he was steered to a notorious tavern that was a hangout for black thugs, and the scene of numerous shootings. In an incongruous linkup, Willard, the roughneck white man, teamed with a black man named Manuel Lee Robinson. He was 28, a 10th grade dropout, and recently released from the Indiana State Reformatory where he had been serving time for burglary.

During the first week of May, 1977, they hit her residence on five consecutive nights. She was not at home the first four times, but on the fifth night (May 6) she was there and surprised them. She was wearing a robe and pajama bottoms. They shot her in the abdomen with a 22-caliber rifle. She died on the kitchen floor. One or both of the men returned before dawn the next morning and set fire to the house in an attempt to conceal their crime.

The FBI and the Indianapolis police believed the pair had taken close to $6 million, giving the pair a record of sorts—perpetrators of the largest robbery in United States history. But they left behind almost that much.

After Mrs. Jackson's body was discovered and the fire that destroyed the center section of the house and roof had been extinguished, the police were shocked at what they found. Money—more than $5 million—was stashed throughout the house. They found money in closets, suitcases, toolboxes and 10 drawers of a vanity in her bathroom. A large plastic garbage container in her bedroom was jammed with bundles of bills, mostly in $100 denominations.

They also found dozens of cakes, many bearing cards with such inscriptions as, "To God, From Marjorie." They found 50 loaves of bread, 200 dozen cookies, 150 pounds of coffee, and in a bedroom thousands of small items wrapped in aluminum foil. They, too, carried inscriptions "To God, From Marjorie." One that was opened contained 15 new washcloths.

Mrs. Jackson was certainly an unusal personality.

Robinson's brief career as a millionaire ended two days after Mrs. Jackson's body was discovered. He and a companion, John A. Williams, 38, a streetwise convict, were spotted buying and pricing a collection of Lincoln automobiles just hours after the first break-in. They aroused the suspicion of dealers, who notified authorities who put them under surveillance. They and Robinson's girlfriend, Annie K. Young, were arrested on the night of May 9. Police confiscated $1.6 million in the homes of Robinson and Miss Young. They also found a paper sack filled with Mrs. Jackson's jewelry.

Miss Young recounted to police that Willard and Mrs. Pollitt showed up at her apartment at 4 a. m. on the morning they torched the house and returned two hours later with toolboxes, suitcases and bags, all filled with money. She said they divided the money with Robinson and then left.

After his arrest, an irate Robinson complained to the police that "someone ripped me off of $72,000." He had left it in a suitcase under a bed in his home. The savvy Williams was quick to deal with the police and tipped them off that Robinson was concealing money even inside the jail. Sure enough, during a shakedown, Robinson reached into his shorts and pulled out a leather folder stuffed with new $100 and $50 bills, and extracted another $300 from his socks.

Willard wasted little time spending some of his share. He bought a 1977 Lincoln Mark IV with a $12,000 check and $3,000 in cash on the day following the first break-in. He wrecked it two days later in Indianapolis. In his favorite tavern in Mooresville, he bragged about being a millionaire, buying drinks for the house and doling out hefty tips.

He and his wife then left for Georgia in their 1972 Oldsmobile pulling a large camper. They picked up Pollitt's sister, Mrs. Robertina Harroll, 53, and her 10-year-old son, Timmy, in their home in Ringgold, Georgia, and headed west.

Life as millionaires for Willard and Mrs. Pollitt ended on May 20 when they were arrested at Tempe, Arizona, after paying $35,515 in cash for a motor home. The sales manager became suspicious and alerted authorities. When they were arrested in a trailer park, FBI agents found they had $170,745 in $100, $50 and $20 bills. Four days later Mrs. Harroll was arrested back in Georgia at Acworth, a town 25 miles northwest of Atlanta. She had purchased a $21,000 trailer in Arizona. FBI agents found $148,000 inside the trailer.

Mrs. Pollitt was quick to cooperate to escape being charged as an accessory in the murder of Mrs. Jackson. She led investigators from the prosecutor's office to a bridge spanning White River not far from Mooresville and said that was where the murder weapon was tossed. Later that day she was flown to Arizona where she led FBI agents to a spot in the desert where they dug down two feet and came up with two cardboard boxes that contained $1,673,460. A total of $3,571,082 of the Jackson heist was recovered but there was strong suspicion that $1 million to $2 million was still missing.

Mrs. Jackson died with an old will that left all of her possessions to her husband and, as a result, the will was null. Her half sister, with whom she had been on the outs since their mother had died in 1969, was the recipient of the estate, estimated at $9 million, though more than half of it went to the Federal government in taxes.

In an ironic footnote, Carolyn Pickering said that years later she met Herbert Biddle at a social function and he told her indignantly, "You're the one who ruined my career."

¤

The robbers and murderers as they appeared in a montage in a Saturday Evening Post *story Connor wrote are (clockwise) Marjorie S. Pollitt and Howard R. Willard, Annie K. Young, John A. Williams, Manuel Lee Robinson, Robertina Harroll.*

38 • Padding My Income

Like many newspapermen on the staff, I did some moonlighting to augment my income in the early years at the paper. So long as we didn't write or report for any publication that was in competition with *The Star*, management didn't object.

When Dow Jones, publisher of the *Wall Street Journal*, decided to start a national weekly newspaper in 1962, they looked for part-time correspondents in most of the states. I was asked if I would be interested in being the Indiana correspondent. I was interviewed by Barney Kilgore, the former DePauw University graduate who started the *Journal*, and Don Carter, editor of the paper named the *National Observer*.

It was an outstanding paper with an excellent staff, mostly reporters and editors from the *Journal*. They reported on the major stories, usually looking for the answer to "why" it happened. Correspondents supplied them with brief, offbeat feature items, and now and then local input on a national story. I wrote a few lengthy stories for the paper, mainly take-offs on stories that we had published.

The *Observer* had a loyal following but it was never able to show a decent profit, so Dow Jones stopped publication after 15 years. Many of its desk editors went back to the *Journal* and several moved on to other papers, some of them as top editors. The pay was decent for the small amount of time I spent on *Observer* stories.

I also reworked some local crime stories for such garish detective magazines as *Startling Detective, Detective Dragnet* and *True Police*. Those magazines liked all the gore in words and pictures they could get. I sometimes wrote under the pseudonym Charles Lawrence.

I reworked the story about Marjorie Jackson and how a pair of robbers murdered her in her home and walked away with $6 million. I pitched it to the *Saturday Evening Post*, and was told that its rate was $300 to $400 for major articles, for which this one qualified. After accepting the story, the managing editor, a young woman, called to tell me that the magazine had a policy of paying only $150, if the article had to be edited. I knew she was embarrassed in telling me that. I seethed for a couple of days but finally agreed, expecting some major changes. When the story appeared in the November 1977 issue one word had been changed.

The *Star Magazine*, our Sunday supplement, ran some of my stories, and if the family vacationed in an interesting locale, I could usually write a story for the paper's travel section. I even submitted items to "Ripley's

Believe It Or Not" until they quit paying for them.

I enjoyed moonlighting. It didn't make me rich, but it allowed me to report and write while I was tied to a desk editing at *The Star*.

¤

39 • *The Star* Wins A Pulitzer

In the summer of 1973 Harley R. Bierce, a general assignment reporter, came to me and suggested the paper form an investigative team. I liked the idea because some of the other major papers had been using them successfully. While a lot of our reporting could have been considered investigative, this would be the first time we set up a full-time team.

Harley talked to Dick Cady about possible subjects to investigate—mental hospitals, prisons, police and organized crime. When Bill Anderson, a veteran police reporter, said he thought the police department would make a promising target, the three of them came to me in August with a proposal to investigate corruption in the department. I gave them two weeks to see what they could discover.

After a couple of weeks they had gathered enough information about massage parlors in the city for an eight-part series, but they also had come up with other information about corruption in the department that warranted further investigating. The trio and photographer Jerry Clark spent the next six months questioning more than 400 persons.

After a few weeks it became obvious that the corruption went beyond the police department, so we wanted the FBI brought in to investigate the corruption that the team had unearthed. Cady and I made a trip to Washington, D. C. to talk to Henry Petersen, assistant attorney general in charge of the criminal division in the Department of Justice. We urged Petersen to authorize the FBI to enter the investigation because we realized that we would get little cooperation from local law enforcement officials. Petersen was skeptical. He said the Justice Department had more important jobs than looking into the problems in a local police department, and he questioned whether it was even within the FBI's jurisdiction. But Cady impressed him with the amount of information the team had already gathered, and convinced him that we'd get no help from the Marion County Prosecutor, Noble R. Pearcy, who was part of the problem. Finally, Petersen agreed to send in agents from the strike force in Chicago. We felt the trip had paid off.

In a memo that I sent down the hall to Pulliam in February two weeks before the series began, I wrote in part:

> More than 400 persons have been questioned. Twenty-seven policemen have come forward only because we gave them assurances that the paper would hold fast. Their jobs and even lives are on the line.

> The FBI has been given access to most—but not all—of our material and been at it for three weeks, interviewing cops and criminals.
>
> What we have shows unbelievable corruption, starting with (Winston L.) Churchill (police chief) on down. Most of the cops who have agreed to testify in a grand jury hearing are young guys who hate the corruption all around them.
>
> I might add, too, that we've learned the nearly two dozen FBI agents working on this are amazed at what they are learning and how blatant is the corruption.
>
> As an example of how corrupt the brass is down there, we have on tape from a whore that she was wired by the police and sent out to get cops cooperating with us in compromising positions. This one is a sodomist (sic) who has bragged that she has dealt with half the force. And her account of being wired was substantiated by a policeman.

In another memo that I wrote, I mentioned that we were being warned that "we were bucking something big, that we'd get hurt…All sorts of rumors…that 37 Federal agents had been here since early February, that the chief would resign, that our phones are tapped, and there was discussion about moving the team's families out of their homes (they weren't). But Anderson did change his home phone number."

It was almost like a movie in the office with Gene, Early, Cady and I gathered around my desk talking about the stories. Tips of all kinds were pouring in. I even checked my car one night to see if it had been wired. I didn't know what I was looking for but the grimy engine didn't appear to be touched, so I drove home.

The paper rented a room in the Hilton Hotel overlooking Ohio Street across from a pawnshop. Jerry Clark camped there for four days during the week before Christmas. He photographed a parade of policemen leaving the pawnshop with television sets, radios and stereos. One shot showed Chief Churchill walking out with a suit of clothes over his shoulder. The shop technically was owned by Morty Dock's father, but Morty ran it. He was generally known to have influence with the cops.

Clark recalled the day that he and Bierce were photographing a policeman going in and out of a barbershop at 34th Street and Fairfield Avenue. As a car came to a stop, the cop would appear to be issuing a ticket but he was exchanging envelopes. Clark said he and Bierce became alarmed when they noticed an unmarked police car with two detectives inside observing them. "We've got to get out of here," Clark recalled Harley saying. They took off and the detectives followed. At Harley's suggestion, Jerry drove north to Fort Harrison, Federal property where the police lacked jurisdiction. When they drove into the fort, the detectives stopped, turned around and left.

Clark said he and his family became frightened by the work, especially the day they discovered the windshield of their car had been smashed. Clark said he called the police to his house to make a report. "They just laughed at me," Clark said. But they filed a report.

For several months the team worked 10 and 12 hours a day, often because many of their sources preferred meeting late in the evenings. They had to be careful about being followed, having their phones tapped, and worrying about sources being wired to trap them. After each interview Cady would sit down and type their notes and place them in a locked file cabinet. We alerted the guards to watch for any strangers in the newsroom after the staff had left for the night.

Overriding those fears was one that hovered over the entire project. Would the publisher order the investigation scrapped because it might have an adverse effect on Mayor Richard G. Lugar's campaign for the U.S. Senate?

In fact, a month before the series began Early said that Pulliam planned to kill the project, saying that he was worried that it would hurt Lugar's Senate run. I talked to his son, Gene, and he said Early misunderstood; that we would run the stories.

But on the day before the series was to begin reporter Bill Shaw answered the phone about 11 a.m. The operator said she needed Lugar's home phone number because Pulliam in Phoenix wanted to talk to him. We expected the worst but about 4 p. m. Early called and when I told him about the call that morning, he said it was likely that Pulliam wanted to invite Lugar to the Gridiron Party in Washington. We heard no more about those fears until two days after the series broke on February 24. Gene came to the page one conference and said his father told him we were doing a good job. It was the first time that the old man had been alerted to the probe. We were amazed that Gene had not told his father about it. "I didn't want to appear to be running to him,"Gene said.

The series started on Sunday, February 24. The stories covered a wide range of topics—prostitution, bootlegging, narcotics, gambling and other areas, as well as cops providing protection for some burglars and fences. The reporters were aided by 28 policemen and eight sheriff's deputies, each of whom broke the "code of silence." Later, another 21 policemen came forward with information. Each was given a code name. Each interview was conducted by two reporters. When possible, the interviews were taped. The team talked to approximately 75 policemen, some retired policemen and hundreds of prostitutes, pimps, junkies, criminals, and victims of the corruption. Each story was carefully reviewed for accuracy for fear of libel suits.

In early March Clark was reassigned to regular photo duties and Myrta Pulliam, Gene's daughter, joined the team.

There was no letup after the series broke. Reaction to the series, the cursory investigations that followed and stories about the controversies kept the team busy.

The series had a remarkable affect on the team. Cady, 34 years old, always the noncommitted, became aggressive, a tough man with a cause. "We've got to win," he kept repeating. Cady was always the skeptical realist who took nothing for granted. In the years that followed, he was called on to reorganize a somnolent drama department, and later became a demanding city editor. A restless, somewhat temperamental sort, Dick was always ready for a change. After leaving the paper in 1999 at the age of 58, he became a free-lance writer and novelist.

Bierce, 33, the staff philosopher, was the team member who was the most articulate and enthused, but Harley's moods were erratic. He was a man with vision, but the rainbow always seemed just beyond his reach.

Anderson, 49, was the plodder. He remained optimistic even when his friends in the police department turned their backs on him when he showed up at headquarters. Bill was the quintessential police reporter. He loved the action, the variety and he also liked cops.

All three of them had left the paper at different times over the years, but each returned before they formed the investigating team. Bill and Harley are deceased and Dick is now a published novelist. Ironically, Harley's son, Benjamin Bierce, is an Indianapolis Police Department patrolman.

The morale of the staff soared after the series got underway. Other reporters were enlisted to handle many of the phone calls that poured into the city room from persons with tips and opinions.

About the time the investigation was losing its momentum, the team put together a series on corruption in police departments in nine major cities. The same corruption problems in the department in Indianapolis showed up in each of the cities.

Cady said the IPD series brought about four investigations; one by the FBI, another an internal probe by the police department, a Marion County grand jury, and one by a new prosecutor who defeated the reigning prosecutor in an election landslide

The stories resulted overall in 56 indictments, including 14 police officers. Of those, three were convicted, three acquitted, and the other cases dismissed. Numerous financial systems (including the police auction, "coffee can fund" and pension system) were improved. Mayor Lugar replaced Chief Churchill and several of his aides, and he accepted the resignation of Public Safety Director William A. Leak.

In a surprise development, Cady and Anderson were indicted on charges of conspiracy to commit a felony (bribery of a policeman). The indictments on September 12 followed a series of stories critical of Prosecutor Noble R. Pearcy. The indictments brought on strong criticism of Pearcy and the grand jury, and it also brought this order from Early eight days later:

> It's imperative that we get definite, provable information that Pearcy has expressed hatred toward *The Star* and its reporters. We need to prove animosity to get a special prosecutor.
>
> Have him observed at his daily luncheons at the Lamplighter or wherever he eats. Observers (at least two at a time) should be close enough to get recordings of his statements.
>
> Have him observed at race tracks. Get art of him at the pari-mutuel windows, especially the $50 one.

This was one of the memos that got spiked.

There was so much criticism of Pearcy from the public and other news outlets that when he ran for re-election in November of that year he was defeated by the largest margin ever suffered by an incumbent in Marion County and Lugar lost his bid for the Senate to Birch Bayh, but was elected two years later.

Charges against Cady and Anderson were dismissed in February, 1975. Those months of hard work and pressure paid off for the team and *The Star.*

The paper won 18 awards including six national ones—the Pulitzer Prize,

National Headliners Award, George Polk Award, Drew Pearson Award, Sigma Delta Chi medal, and AP Freedom of Information Award.

The Investigative Reporters and Editors organization (IRE) grew out of the investigative team. Harley and Myrta wanted a national organization that would allow newspapers to share information and reporting techniques. They did most of the seed work with Paul Williams of Ohio State. IRE was founded in 1976 and now has 3,000 members.

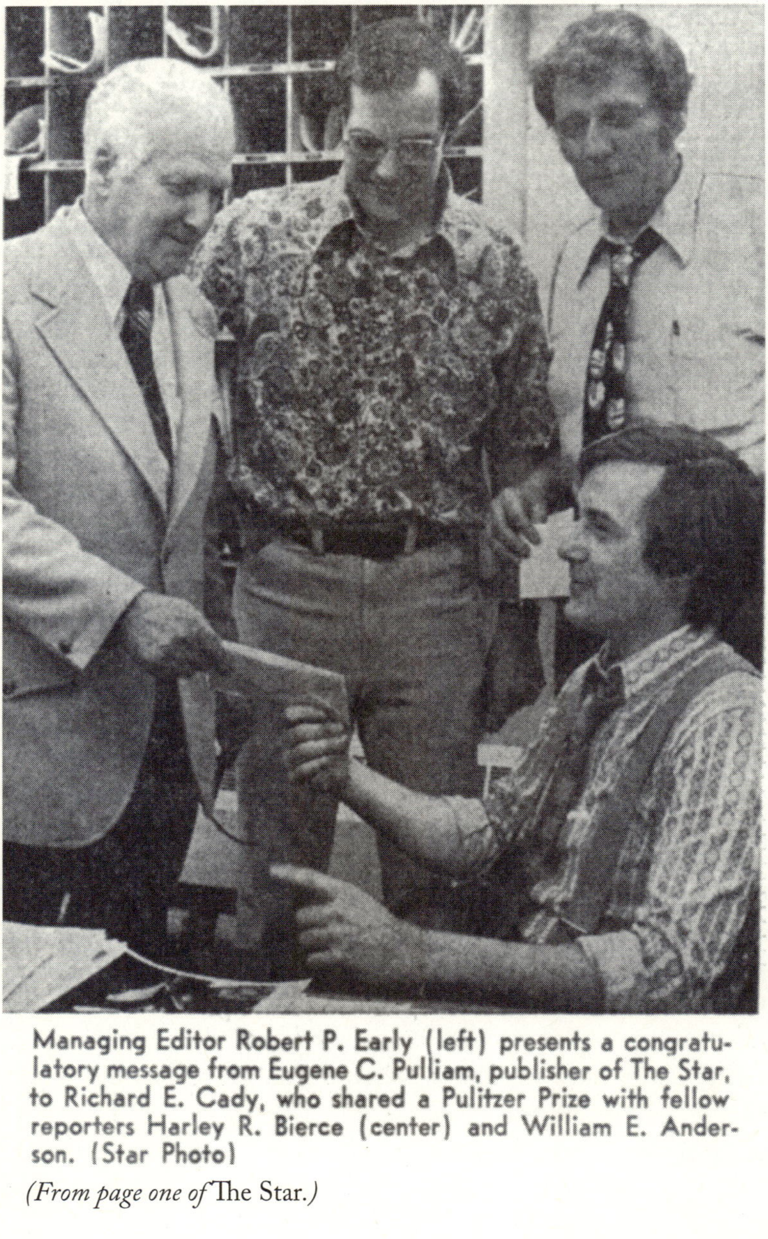

Managing Editor Robert P. Early (left) presents a congratulatory message from Eugene C. Pulliam, publisher of The Star, to Richard E. Cady, who shared a Pulitzer Prize with fellow reporters Harley R. Bierce (center) and William E. Anderson. (Star Photo)

(From page one of The Star.*)*

40 • We Win A Second Pulitzer

We learned from the investigation of the police department that it takes a lot of time, money, brains and enterprise to win a Pulitzer Prize, especially the prize for investigative reporting. The subject has to be of sufficient importance to justify spending months gathering information, but in the early stages of any investigation it's difficult to estimate how much time and manpower it will require. It tends to sneak up on you.

When Joseph T. Hallinan began looking into medical malpractice in the state prisons in June of 1989, he had no idea where it would eventually lead him. When he went to the state's Department of Insurance for information one day, a clerk steered him in another direction. She told him that some of the physicians with the most malpractice claims against them weren't working in the prison system. They were in private practice. So Hallinin, 29, a member of *The Star* staff since graduating from Boston University five years earlier, began the process of going through reports about malpractice in the private sector.

"There were a small number of doctors who had lost multiple malpractice suits, and they suffered no form of punishment," Hallinan said. "They didn't lose their licenses, nor did they have to undergo any retraining or re-education...in some cases the malpractice insurance premiums didn't increase."

Four months into the investigation we teamed Susan Headden, 35, with Hallinan to help in the expanding investigation. Linda Caleca, an editor who directed the project, said Hallinan was dogged in his pursuit of facts, and Headden was brought on to help get the work done quicker. She was also an excellent writer.

The pair spent the better part of a year working on the story. They investigated physicians who maimed and mutilated scores of patients in Indiana with little or no discipline from the state or the medical associations. The result of their work was a comprehensive three-part series that ran in *The Star* in June of 1990 and earned the paper its second Pulitzer Prize.

The medical profession has such an aura of trust and almost sacredness that the reporters had to be exact in what they wrote. They used no anonymous sources. Just about every word in the series was gone over carefully by editors, and, in some cases, by attorneys.

Once they got to the stage of talking to victims of the malpractice, they said it became depressing writing about people who had lost legs and breasts and had lost their children. Some patients became deaf and disabled. Some botched surgeries required amputations. Some patients died as a result of poor treatment. Headden said:

> Things got sort of tense at the end, with the pressure of using names of doctors. You're aware of the impact you could have on someone's reputation.
>
> It was a very depressing story to work on. Every day you had to immerse yourself in these tragedies.
>
> It's the kind of journalism we should do more of. But the fact that it took a year shows it's hard.

The series impressed the Pulitzer judges but it didn't have much effect in medical circles in Indiana.

Both reporters and the paper had hoped that the work would have a beneficial affect on the health-care system, but they saw no such effect.

"So far, zip, nothing," Hallinan said after receiving the award. "The system is still the same as it was before the articles, primarily due to agreement between the three powerful special interest groups that have control over malpractice legislation in Indiana." Those three are doctors, trial lawyers and the insurance industry—a formidable group.

Both reporters left the paper, Hallinan in 1991 for "more money and opportunity, the same reason everybody leaves, I guess," he said. He went to the Washington Bureau of Newhouse News Service where he started writing about prisons. He spent a year at Harvard University as a Nieman Fellow in 1997-98 where he did research for a book about the growth of prisons in the U.S. The book, *Going Up the River*, was published by Random House in 2001 and subsequently was named a *New York Times* notable book.

He wrote the book he said "because, while at Newhouse, I began to see this astonishing transformation in the American prison system. I also saw that virtually no one else was paying attention to it: I had it all to myself! So I started documenting how the get-tough-on-crime legislation that was being passed around the country was filling up prisons, and how the prisons were transforming the places where they were built and the people who worked in them."

He currently reports for the *Wall Street Journal* in the Chicago bureau.

Headden joined *U. S. News and World Report* weekly magazine where she currently is one of its top editors.

It was time for a toast for reporters Susan M. Headden and Joseph T. Hallinan, winners of the Pulitzer Prize for investigative reporting.

STAR STAFF PHOTO
KELLY WILKINSON

41 • A Benign Publisher

There was a lot less turmoil at the paper when Eugene S. Pulliam—"Young Gene"—became the publisher after his father died in Phoenix in 1975. While he had been overseeing the two papers from his office just down the hall from the two newsrooms for 13 years as assistant publisher, there was never any question of who was the ultimate boss. It was ECP.

In fact, there were occasions when Bob Early referred to Gene as "the kid." And I remember one afternoon when I was having trouble lobbying Bill Dyer for more space for a major project that I bolstered my position by mentioning that Gene (then the publisher) had okayed it. That wasn't enough to convince Dyer. His response: "Gene's a wimp." Gene might not bluster, but he was no wimp.

Perhaps they remembered Gene as the young man who came back from four years in the Navy and went to work as the *Star's* aviation editor, a position I can't remember ever being filled after Gene gave it up to become an assistant city editor. In 1948 he became managing editor of *The News*.

He was no shouter. He was quiet and polite but could be firm. One afternoon in his office when I referred to a city councilman as a "son of a bitch," he stopped me and said, "Now we don't need to use that kind of language." I wonder what he said to Bob Early when Early got rolling on one of his obscenity-laced tirades?

I learned up close how Gene operated in the three months that I served as editor of the editorial page in 1979. I liked writing editorials telling the White House how to handle matters; realizing full well that Washington was a thousand miles away and not really concerned with advice from *The Indianapolis Star*. Once I knocked out a brief editorial calling for the U. S. to invade some banana republic in Latin America. Gene read the galley proof and told me, "It's a good idea but maybe we should sit on it for a day or two." It's still sitting.

There was a time when I bought into a recommendation of an alcohol counselor (a former copy editor) that the only way we could cure Bob Collins, the sports editor, of a serious drinking problem was to fire him. I discussed the idea with Gene, who quietly said he didn't think that was such a good idea. He was right, of course. It was a lousy idea. But Collins, a good friend, kept on drinking.

It was reassuring to work with a publisher who had a lot of common sense, and to know that he would take your side against his father if he thought you were right.

Quiet and modest, Gene gave advice only after being asked. He insisted on fairness and accuracy in the news reporting. He rarely interfered with the operation of the newsroom, but he always checked the editorial page proofs. While his father never showed up in the newsroom, Gene was always just a few steps from it in his office down the hall.

Most of the staff members called him Gene. When a new reporter joined the paper, he would often drop by and introduce himself. If he particularly liked a story or headline, he would send a crisp new $2 bill to the reporter or copy editor. But other than that bit of largesse, he was close with the corporation's dollars, rarely ever approving more than ten dollars for a weekly merit raise. In that respect, he took his cues from Bill Dyer. But whenever the bean counters recommended that the paper charge for obituaries, Gene always nixed it. "People get mentioned in the paper only when they are born and when they die," he said, "so we're not going to charge them for dying."

Something of a loner, he usually left the office at noon and walked across University Park to have two martinis and lunch at the Indianapolis Athletic Club. He would sit alone at regular table by a window and read.

Gene avoided the limelight and was uncomfortable when called upon to give an address or even make a few remarks at a gathering. He didn't like to pose for photographs, either. And while he made sure that the editorial page reflected his conservatism, Gene did not impose his views in the news columns. That freed the staff to pursue news without wondering if it conflicted with his political views.

I always wondered how he felt about his father. Was he embarrassed about his father's demands that the paper reflect his views? And did he feel intimidated by the man? He never gave any indication of how he felt. Always the loyal and obedient son.

Away from the office, he was active in the Episcopal Church and served on local boards and national journalism organizations. He had been one of the state's top amateur golfers, and he held offices in the United States Golf Association, golf's ruling body. He died in 1999 at age 84.

My favorite story about Gene came from Tom Crowe, at that time general manager of the two papers. Tom said he was upset that the papers had not met its budget projections on one of those years when the economy was doing poorly. He told Gene how he felt and he said that Gene replied, "Don't worry about it, Tom. We had a good year last year and we'll have a good year next year."

(l-r) Harvey Jacobs, Editor of The News; *E. S. Pulliam, Casper Weinberge, Secretary of Defense; Lawrence Connor, Frank Coperton, then Managing Editor of* The News; *and John H. Lyst, Editorial Page Editor of* The Star.

42 • We All Wrote Obits

Mike Horrell, a brash young reporter, liked to tell other young reporters, "If you smoke a pipe and carry a briefcase, you don't have to write obits."

He was wrong, of course, because just about everybody on the staff wrote obits. Cub reporters began their careers writing obituaries, and even seasoned reporters at times were called upon to churn out an obit or two in a pinch

It didn't take an advanced degree to write an obituary. Most of them followed a standard formula. We emphasized accuracy. We knew that families pasted obituaries in albums and an error was always an irritant. We knew, too, that an obituary likely was the last time the decedent would get mentioned in the paper.

Whoever was running the city desk would look for a person of some prominence to feature as the lead obit on the page; one warranting a one or two-column headline. It was standard procedure for the reporter to check with the morgue (the paper's library) for information and a photo about a suitable candidate. There were days when it was a stretch to find anyone of note to feature. It still is and that's why the obit with the headline might be some 93-year-old physicist from Newark or an aged songwriter from Malibu.

Just about any local person of note—an executive, politician, architect, lawyer, professor, judge or clergyman—who turned 70 or was known to be ailing became a candidate for a prepared obit. We must have had a hundred or more prepared obits on file at any one time ready to be pulled from a filing cabinet when the person left us. Some even qualified for photo layouts on their lives. The wire services regularly sent out prepared obits on major newsmakers.

Our reporters were encouraged to look for an element in the decedent's life to feature in the lead paragraph of the obit, but it had to have been of some significance. Not so for Bess Watson, the longtime obit writer for *The News*. She relentlessly queried families for some element in the decedent's life. If the person saved bottle caps, the obit would begin:

"Sadie Thompson spent 23 years saving bottle caps.

"When she died yesterday she had 1,322 caps in her collection…"

Governor Roger D. Branigin said that his only fear of dying was that Bess would write his obit.

Perhaps, Branigin, a Democrat, noted what she had to say about one of her subjects: "Although a lifelong Republican, he was known as a man of integrity."

Reporters were warned to be careful taking obits over the phone. Pranksters thought it amusing to knock off a friend in the paper. Generally, reporters would spot the calls as fake because the callers weren't able to supply routine facts about the person.

One exception came when we reported the death of a local attorney, Earl Capehart, the son of a former U. S. Senator Homer Capehart. He didn't raise hell about our knocking him off prematurely, but he did call to insist we straighten out the record the next day.

We never learned who had planted the obit, but the managing editor decreed that from then on all obits had to come from the funeral home or be confirmed there.

We didn't usually include the cause of a person's death but if we learned it was due to suicide it was mentioned; that is until the morning I got a telephone call from a friend about the obit we ran on his brother. We mentioned that his brother had committed suicide. The distraught brother said the family in Indianapolis was distressed about it and that he could not understand why it had to be mentioned. After mulling it over later, I thought the complaint was valid, so I issued an order that henceforth routine obits would not include the cause of death.

¤

43 • A Gruesome Crime

We'd seen our share of gore, abuse, violence and murder but none quite like what happened to a 16-year-old girl in the fall of 1965.

Her name was Sylvia Likens, a slender, pretty girl with a sassy look but otherwise with an unassuming manner. She maintained average grades in school but she was frequently absent, and finally dropped out when she reached 16.

Sylvia and her sister, Jenny, 15, were left by their parents with a virtual stranger while they went on tour with a carnival in July of that year. Jenny wore a metal leg brace as a result of a bout with polio. The "caregiver" was Gertrude Baniszewski, who lived in half of a dingy, gray double at 3850 East New York Street with five of her seven children in a neighborhood that was on its way to becoming a slum.

Life had not been kind to Gertrude. She was 37 but looked to be 50. She had 13 pregnancies and six miscarriages. She, too, had quit school at 16, married John Baniszewski and bore him four children. She divorced him after 10 years, but after three unhappy months married to a man while living in Kansas, she left and returned to Indianapolis and lived with Baniszewski for another seven years. That second union produced two more children.

She divorced him again in 1963 and began cohabiting with a young lover, Dennis Lee Wright. She bore him a son before he deserted her.

At the age of 37 Gertrude had been abused by her husbands, and suffered from asthma, bronchitis and nervous tension, all aggravated by chain smoking. It didn't help that the house had become a noisy, chaotic hangout for neighborhood children.

This was the woman charged with caring for the Likens girls. Their parents, Lester and Betty Likens, paid $20 a week for their care. Gertrude took in ironing and did some babysitting to eke out a living to help pay the monthly rent of $55 and to buy groceries for her family. There was never enough food. The eldest daughter, Paula, 17, helped support the family by sharing her earnings from her job at a cafeteria.

Three months after moving in with the Baniszewskis, Sylvia was dead; the victim of steady brutality over a three-week period. Led by Gertrude, she and some of her children and neighborhood children carried out a systematic torture that took Sylvia's life.

The evening that she died police found her lying on a mattress on the floor of a second-story bedroom. Until that night she had been sleeping on a pile of rags in the basement. When police arrived on report of a death at the house, they found a girl with the words, "I'M A PROSTITUTE AND PROUD OF IT' carved on her midriff with a needle. A large numeral "3" was deeply branded on her chest. Her body was bruised, and covered with open sores, cuts, burns, and more than 100 small round sores—each about the size of a cigarette burn. Her lips were in shreds and her fingernails had been bent backwards.

Near the end of her ordeal police later learned that she had been fed urine and excrement. On at least one occasion she had been tied up and dropped in a bathtub of scalding water. At other times her tormentors had gathered around while she sat naked on the floor with a soft drink bottle inserted in her vagina. They struck her with paddles and broomsticks. Paula Baniszewski, who weighed 160 pounds, had bragged about breaking her own wrist when she hit Sylvia in the mouth. After she got a cast on her hand, she went back to hitting Sylvia in the face.

In reconstructing the crime, police discovered that Sylvia had been beaten, tortured and starved over a three-week period by a dozen or more people, mostly teen-agers. She became the victim of mob psychology with family members and neighbor children taking turns in tormenting the docile girl until it went much farther than any of them could have imagined.

Just why she was targeted became something of a mystery. Some said Gertrude might have been jealous of the attractive young woman. She favored young men herself and may have regarded Sylvia as a rival.

The victim was no angel. She liked the boys and she was frequently absent from school, but she was also religious and regularly attended services with Jenny. The other children became convinced that she was spreading rumors about their sexual activities. Gertrude insisted that Sylvia was pregnant, which was untrue. She frequently lashed out at the girl, shouting, "I hate you. I hate you."

Sylvia was a docile sort and neither she nor her sister reported the abuse to their parents on the rare times they showed up. Fear seemed to rule both of the girls. Jenny escaped the torture her sister was undergoing.

First-degree murder indictments were returned against Gertrude, daughters Paula and Stephanie, and her son Johnny, 12, as well as two 15-year-old boys, Coy Hubbard and Richard Hobbs, who frequently hung out at the house.

After a three-week trial, Gertrude was found guilty of first-degree murder. Paula was found guilty of second-degree murder. Johnny Baniszewski and Hubbard and Hobbs were found guilty of manslaughter. The grand jury reconsidered the evidence against Stephanie and set her free.

A *Star* reporter, John Dean, who covered the Likens trial, wrote a book in 1966 about the crime and the trial. He titled it *The Indiana Torture Slaying*. In a foreword, Leroy K. New, the chief trial deputy for the Marion County Prosecutor, wrote:

"In 20 years of practice in the field of law, in serving three prosecutors and handling homicides totaling well over a hundred, I feel that the Likens story has the most ominous moral implications of any story which I have ever been involved in or even heard of."

New told me a few months before he died in 2005 that after Gertrude was sentenced and about to leave the courtroom in handcuffs she asked him, "Will you shake my hand?"

New said, "I told her, 'Gertrude I don't hate you but what you did was abominable.'" He said he shook her hand and she was led away.

New surprised many of those involved in the case by inviting Jenny to live with him, his wife and two daughters. He said she stayed with them about a year. After he set some house rules, New said Jenny settled down and attended North Central High School. They sent her to a school in Maine to learn about operating bank machines. She finished the course and worked in a bank in Indianapolis; later married a truck driver and lived in Texas but eventually came back to Indianapolis. New said she died sometime in 2004.

Forest Bowman, who as a young attorney represented 13-year-old Johnny Baniszewski in the trial, kept track of some of the principals in the case. He said that Johnny became a fundamentalist preacher. Gertrude died a few years after being paroled. Richard Hobbs died of cancer at a young age. Coy Hubbard was convicted of robbery after leaving prison. Both he and New said they had lost track of Paula.

Dean in his book mentioned that Paula was finding life in the Indiana Women's Prison comfortable. It was the nicest bed she ever had, she told her attorney.

For several years Bowman said that he received a telephone call at 2 a.m. each year on the anniversary of Sylvia's death. "The caller would say something like, 'You remember Sylvia, don't you?'" he said. Bowman said he guessed it was a way of reminding him that he had represented one of her killers. "I'd listen, hang up the phone and go back to sleep."

After leaving *The Star*, John Dean changed his name to Natty Bumppo, a name made famous in James Fenimore Cooper's *The Leatherstocking*

Tales, a series of five novels published between 1823 and 1841. I guess he just admired Natty, the hero in the books. His account of the Likens case was printed as a pocketbook and sold for 75 cents. I recently saw a battered copy of it in an antique mall. It was priced at $65.

∞ ∞ ∞

It's not often that we had two major local stories break on the same day, but it happened the day Sylvia died. We had planned to break a major story the night that Sylvia's body was found. It was an exposé about a Marion County sheriff's deputy reportedly beating a prisoner to death in the county jail. Reporter Rick Johnson had been working on the story for 11 weeks. It was based mainly on the statements of Charles P. McAdams, a prisoner who allegedly witnessed the beating. But Sheriff Bob Fields contended the victim had been beaten to death by a mental patient who shared the cell with him.

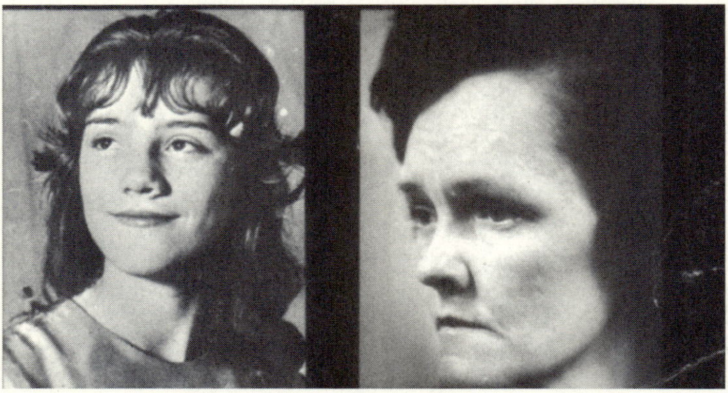

Sylvia Likens (l) andGertrude Baniszewski.

The exposé ran as the lead story through all three editions of the paper. When the police found Sylvia's body early that evening, we hurriedly put together a bulletin about it in the first edition. In the second edition we had enough information for an incomplete story, and by the final edition we published a more complete story with photographs of Sylvia and Hobbs.

I never doubted that the Likens story got more attention from readers than the exposé about the beating in the jail, but both stories dominated page one for several days.

Unfortunately, the exposé lost some of its luster when McAdams, an alcoholic, was given a bottle of whiskey in his jail cell. We never learned who gave him the bottle but suspected it was someone on the sheriff's payroll. A liquored McAdams retracted his accusation. And the sheriff subsequently sued the paper for libel.

We lost the suit and were fined $10,000. Jurors said they felt it necessary to recommend the fine because Johnson during his investigation got into an argument with Sheriff Fields in a City-County Building hallway and blurted, "I'm going to get you." Witnesses confirmed that they heard the threat.

It was the only libel suit we lost in the 41 years I worked at the paper. There had been several suits and threats of suits, but none that we ever lost. And very few went to trial.

¤

44 • Rumors of Terrorism

We received periodic rumors of terrorists poised to strike in the city. They proved to be unfounded, but there was general unrest and anger among blacks throughout the country in the 1960s and 1970s. Many had rioted in dozens of cities, causing widespread damage.

There was general concern across the country that blacks might stage riots during the nation's Bicentennial.

I received a note from Bob Early dated January 2, 1976. It read:

> Eldridge Cleaver is reported to have come back to the United States for one purpose:
>
> To participate in a nationwide movement to train black guerrillas, culminating in attacks on cities throughout the nation in July.
>
> It is to be known as "The Black Revolution Massacre." According to rumors:
>
> It is planned to wipe out the whites in cities just as the Indians did in settlements.
>
> Tactics will include hit-and-run terrorist bombings similar to the bombing at LaGuardia Airport.
>
> Initial targets will be police departments, local and state throughout the nation, and National Guard units from coast to coast.
>
> Meanwhile, it is said that the Pentagon has not released truthful figures about the number of machineguns, M-16 rifles, mortars, small rocket launchers, grenade launchers and small arms that have been stolen from National Guard armories over the last several years.
>
> These are just rumors, of course, but I am sending similar information to Ben Cole [our Washington correspondent], so he can look into matters at his end.

A week later I received another note with more specifics. It read:

> Concerning the start of the "Black Revolution" said to be scheduled to start July 4:
>
> An arsenal of all types of weapons is being built up in all directions from 30th and Meridian streets.
>
> A 'death list' has been prepared which includes the names

> of 100 Indianapolis policemen. Among them are top Negro policemen labeled "Uncle Toms."
>
> The plans of the leaders include taking over radio and television simultaneously, also grab the newspapers..
>
> They also plan to take over police headquarters. [Plans to take over the telephone company were scratched because of "too much security."]
>
> This information came from the same source that reported plans for the "Black Revolution" in all major cities on July 4.
>
> It is time, I believe, to start checking these reports with the Mayor, Police Chief and the Governor to see if they have heard anything and, if so, what are they doing.
>
> This all jells with the statement made by Kelley of the FBI last week that terrorists, he believes, are making revolutionary plans for 1976.

I was a bit skeptical of some of the details, but otherwise took the warnings seriously.

Reporter Rick Johnson was assigned to check out the reports. He talked to more than 50 persons, mostly in law enforcement, but could not confirm the rumors, though there were few outright denials. One of Rick's street sources put it this way: "The blacks here have got it too good to start any real shit. There's all sorts of money out there for them if they want to scuffle for it. If they start that bombin', shootin' an shit the heat comes down so hard no one can move, no one can make a buck."

"Other sources did not put it so concisely," Rick wrote in his memo, "but all agreed there has been some talk."

Sometime during those volatile years, Early decided that the reporters and photographers needed some protection if they were sent out to cover a riot, so we bought a dozen or more metal helmets. We must have believed that rioters would avoid pelting the press with rocks because Early had the helmets painted white with "The Indianapolis Star" painted on the front and "Reporter" or "Photographer" painted on the back. They were never used and the year passed without incident.

I never learned the source of Early's anonymous tips, but wondered if might have come from one of those sycophants who visited him in his office late at night.

45 • The City Shuts Down

There's really only one way to cope with a blizzard: stock up on groceries and stay indoors with a good book or watch television until you can't take any more of the weathermen—and weatherwomen—rehashing forecasts and reports of traffic snarls and church and school closings. Enjoy the day off. It can't last.

But that sort of coping wasn't enough when the worst blizzard in the city's history roared into Indiana on Wednesday afternoon, January 25, 1978, and closed down most of the state for four days, locking parents in their homes with children whose initial excitement vanished when they realized they weren't going anywhere (even outside the front door) for several days. They even began to miss school.

It started mildly enough. On Tuesday evening, a winter storm warning was cancelled and the temperature stood at 36 degrees. On Wednesday morning snow and sleet was falling and a major storm was forecast. The first blizzard warning came at 3:45 p.m. By 6 p.m. the temperature dropped below freezing and winds of 20 miles per hour hit the city. Visibility dropped to three-eighteenths of a mile. At 8:45 p.m. travelers were warned to get off the streets and highways. By 11 p.m. the winds were at 45 mph and they peaked at 55 mph at 2:12 a.m. Thursday.

At 4 a.m. Thursday 13 inches of snow was on the ground, five of it from an earlier snowfall. And still the snow came. It didn't stop until 2:02 a.m. on Friday, but even after that snow fell less than inch each day over the next four days.

On Friday 20 inches of snow was on the ground but the winds had caused drifts of six to eight feet.

The state was paralyzed. Stores and schools were closed for three days. Motorists were stranded. Airports closed. When it was all over 19 persons had died from the storm.

All of this was a challenge for us working at *The Star*. We published a 56-page paper on Wednesday night a few hours after the blizzard struck, but the circulation trucks had difficulty delivering the papers. Twenty-seven of the trucks got snowbound, and only about 20,000 papers were delivered to a normal 132,000 subscribers in Marion County. There was practically no distribution outside the county.

Many of the reporters and editors in the newsroom left early trying to stay ahead of the storm. About a dozen of us spent the night in the nearby Essex House hotel or in the Indianapolis Athletic Club across University

Park. Several of us gathered in the IAC room I had rented after the abbreviated run was completed. I had the foresight to send a copy boy out to a liquor store earlier in the evening, so we partied for an hour or so before the crew trudged through the snow to the Essex House.

When I woke up Thursday morning I looked out of the seventh floor window of the Athletic Club to an eerie, almost surreal, sight. The city was a sea of white. Not a car in sight. Not a person in sight. Snowplows had not yet made an appearance.

The National Weather Service labeled the storm "the worst blizzard in Indiana history." But it wasn't over. The wind chill at 9 a.m. was 51 degrees below zero.

University Park was under nearly 15 inches of snow but I plowed through to get back to the paper. Throughout the day a few other staffers who lived close by drifted in. We had about one third of the normal editorial force, most of them staying downtown over the next three days.

The staff photographers lined up four-wheeled-drive trucks so they could get out to provide photographs for the papers. The reporters worked the phones.

Only about 60 of the normal crew of 600 in the production departments were in the building, working in shifts to produce both *The Star* and *The News.*

There was just enough help to enable us to publish 12-page, ad-free papers on Friday and Saturday mornings. They were delivered downtown. Friday's press run was 25,000 papers.

"I just didn't want to miss an edition as long as there were people there to put it out," Tom Crowe, the general manager, said later.

On Sunday we printed a 40-page paper with some advertising. The Sunday paper then had a statewide circulation of about 370,000. That day we printed 190,000 papers and nearly all of them went to Marion County subscribers.

I spent four nights at the IAC. Airline stewardesses who were marooned in the city volunteered as waitresses there and at downtown hotels. For the first couple of days persons stranded in the club found it novel and exciting. The Four Lads, a musical group that had been booked for a show there on Wednesday night and were among the stranded, put on a casual performance in the dining room on Thursday night.

After a couple of days, the novelty wore off and boredom overtook the millions of Hoosier trapped in hotels and homes for four days.

I finally got home on Sunday afternoon 94 hours after I had left home on Wednesday.

A week later we published a special 16-page section in the Sunday paper recapping the storm and reproducing the front pages of the papers most of the subscribers never saw. Thousands of those sections stored in closets have turned tan waiting for grandchildren to read about the Blizzard of '78.

A tattered newspaper blows across an otherwise deserted Ohio Street in this photo by Star *photographer Jim Ramsey taken on the morning after the blizzard shut down the city.*

46 • A Deadly Scam

When Bob Kellum, the business editor, wrote a column about Stanley A. Selig and his brother Ben purchasing 3,000,000 acres of fertile land in Brazil [SA] in the early 1960s, I thought it looked like a scam in the works. The brothers began selling off parts of the land to suckers believing they were going to own a cattle ranch and make a killing.

"An Invitation To Meet At The Foot Of The Rainbow To Divide The Pot Of Gold" was emblazoned on the cover of a gaudy brochure the brothers had put out touting a fantastic land opportunity in Brazil. Inside were color pictures of land knee-deep in grass and shots of modern government buildings in Brasilia, the nation's new capital.

A friend gave William C. Jones a copy of the brochure. Jones was a 6-foot, 190-pound rough-hewn 46-year-old bachelor living in Anchorage, Alaska. He had been working in Alaska for 11 years as a pipe fitter on an oil line, earning $500 to $900 a week. Bill Jones was ripe for Selig's pitch. He was looking for romance and security. And he knew that the oil boom wouldn't last forever. He envisioned owning and operating a farm and cattle ranch in the lush land promised in the brochure.

Jones was deliberate, mild in speech and appeared unemotional. James E. Rocap, who became his Indianapolis attorney, said, "I asked him once why he never showed any emotion. He told me he had landed on Iwo Jima during the war (World War II) with the second wave of Marines and for eight days and nights he was under fire constantly. The pounding must have been God-awful. He finally got wounded on the eighth day. Jones told me. 'After those eight days nothing else that's happened could shake me.'"

Jones got hooked on the promises in Brazil. He telephoned Stanley Selig to inquire about the opportunities and Selig sent him more literature. By then Selig's brother Ben had dropped out of the operation. Stanley had a reputation as a shady dealer in real estate in the Indianapolis area; most of his victims being poor blacks. But he was smart, and he had a "life master" rating as a bridge player.

In February, 1967, Jones sold a home he maintained in Jonesboro, Arkansas. He mailed Selig a down payment of $2,900 on 16,439 acres at $1.80 an acre. After he made six more payments, he flew to Brazil to look over his land. It took him two days to find the area but he never was sure which land was his. He did notice that the land was barren and rocky, and that there were no roads and the nearest town was 200 miles away.

Jones's doubts began so he confronted Selig in Indianapolis. The slick talking Selig reassured him so he signed a conditional sales contract and agreed to pay Selig $740 a month until the total of $29,000 was paid.

Jones was just one of hundreds of other buyers pouring money into Selig's office situated in a large brick residence on fashionable North Meridian Street, a block from the governor's residence. By then local and Federal officials were starting to warn investors about Selig's prospectus. A new government in Brazil, a military junta, discovered that 14 land buyers from all over the world had purchased land tracts, working with local Brazilian officials. Like Selig, they were selling it off as cattle ranches.

So, in 1969 a new law declared that the transfer of such property was null and void. The law threw Selig into a panic. He began a nationwide campaign for help. The Brazilian government modified the law in 1971 allowing foreign investors to purchase land, provided that within three years from the date of the contract they would establish domicile in Brazil and work the land.

Unaware of the changes, and anxious to begin his new life, Jones flew a second time to Brazil. He was told that the deeds to his land were forged and invalid. He promptly flew to Indianapolis. The date was March 9, 1970. He checked into the York Hotel in downtown Indianapolis, celebrated principally for the porno film theater on the ground floor.

Jones stopped at the Federal Building to lay his case before postal inspectors and U. S. District Attorney Stanley B. Miller. They showed interest and told him to gather documents and return. The next morning he decided to confront Selig. He showed up at the house at 9:30 a. m. and Selig arrived 40 minutes later. They talked. Jones demanded that Selig return his money. The conversation got heated and after 40 minutes, Selig got to his feet, bounded into his secretary's office and told her to call the police.

He went back to his desk, reached in a drawer and pulled out a 40-caliber pistol with a nine-inch barrel and pointed it at Jones. Jones said he backed up and begged him not to shoot and then reached into his suit-coat pocket for a 25-caliber automatic. He later told the police that he fired two shots into Selig and when he kept coming at him, he fired three more. Selig, 52, died at the hospital.

Jones admitted shooting Selig. He was arrested and later freed under a $15,000 bond put up by a cousin who lived in Indianapolis. A grand jury indicted Jones but the only charge was carrying an unregistered weapon. He pleaded guilty and was fined $500 and given a two-year suspended sentence.

But that wasn't the end of it. In the following August, Jones filed a claim against the Selig estate for $50,000. The administrators promptly filed a counter claim for $100,000 in a wrongful death action.

The trial was held in Marion County Probate Court in the last week of January, 1974. The testimony that was never given in a murder trial came out in the probate trial. At the end of the five-day trial, the jury after 80 minutes of deliberation told Probate Judge Edward Madigan that Jones should received $27,132—the exact amount he had paid Selig for the worthless land and taxes connected with the purchase.

After the jury marched in with its verdict, one of the jurors said to Rocap, Jones's attorney, "Why didn't you ask for more?"

Rocap said Jones stayed in Indianapolis until he got his $27,000 and then he returned to Alaska.

"That was the last I ever heard of him," Rocap, now deceased, said.

He remembered other lawyers telling him, "You'll never win that case. What jury would award a guy after he murders a man and then sues his estate to get his money back."

"But we won it," Rocap said chuckling.

William C. Jones ponders his fate.

Stanley Selig was sued after he was buried.

CAN YOU SUE A MAN YOU'VE KILLED ...AND COLLECT?

This headline was in a police magazine story Connor wrote.

¤

47 • Time To Leave

As managing editor, I soon learned that readers have an attachment to comic strips, even when the strips grow old and tired. Whenever we replaced one of the soap opera strips like Mary Worth with a new strip, we could count on spending a day or two listening to complaints, mostly from older readers.

I had not been managing editor many weeks when I pulled my first major blunder. It concerned the comic strip Doonesbury, a target of conservative readers then and now. But the strip has also had a loyal and passionate following from more liberal readers.

A few days before the 1980 presidential election the editor who handled the syndicated features brought me a week's collection of Doonesbury strips he thought that I should see. The sequence centered on Ronald Reagan's brain. The strips were slated to run a few days before the election. It featured TV newsman Roland Hedley asking viewers to join him on a "journey into the unknown—a fantastic voyage through the brain of Ronald Reagan." In the course of the week's strips Hedley reports that a vision disorder left the candidate "only able to see backward through a rose-colored mist." I knew Reaganites would detest it.

The Star had a policy of not publishing letters to the editor critical of any of the candidates in the last week before the election because the target of the attack would not have a chance to respond. As a novice managing editor, I thought I was being a responsible editor if I scrapped the offensive strips and told the readers why we were doing it.

But first I cleared it with the publisher, Gene Pulliam. He agreed that the strips were offensive and told me to do what I thought best. So I told the features editor to scrap the strips that were scheduled to begin running on the following Monday. I printed our rationale of why they were being held out in the space where Doonesbury regularly ran.

It was a poor decision, one that backfired on me and on the paper.

When I got to the office that Monday morning, I was greeted with a telephone call from an angry subscriber. It was the first of hundreds of angry calls. Several of us, including my secretary, the unflappable Mary Ann Wolf, spent most of the day listening patiently to callers hour after hour, accusing the "Republican" paper of censorship and "bitter electioneering." Many demanded that we publish the strips. The newsroom staff was just as irate as the subscribers.

One of the television stations came to the office and interviewed me. The wire services quickly ran a national roundup of papers that reacted to the strips. Some simply took them off of the comic page, and ran them elsewhere in the paper. The sissies! As far as I could learn the only other paper to withhold the strip was the *Daytona Beach Journal.* United Press International quoted me as saying, "Too many readers thought we were being censors and biased, when all we were trying to do was be fair and saw the strips as an unwarranted attack."

"If it was Carter, we'd have done the same thing," I said. It didn't help that the paper had already endorsed Reagan on the editorial page.

Garry Trudeau, the Doonesbury cartoonist, was quoted as saying he was furious at what we had done but he didn't agree that it was censorship.

After nine hours of being lectured, we capitulated and ran the entire series over the next two days on the Op-Ed page rather than on the comic page.

It wasn't the only time that I got battered for killing a feature. And, of course, the problem was politics. During the last week of a senatorial campaign a few years later the staff ran an office poll on which candidate they favored in the election. They voted overwhelmingly for Birch Bayh, the Democrat nominee. Although it was strictly an in-house vote, one of the reporters showed the results to columnist Tom Keating. He proceeded to write his column for the next day's paper on the poll. Since it was the last week of the campaign, we were abiding by the policy of not publishing letters to the editor or editorials for or against a candidate.

I was sure that Tom knew that the paper did not favor Bayh; in fact, the word came down that we were to do whatever we could to see him defeated. After all, he was a Democrat.

I had left the office and was at home when I got a call from the news editor telling me about Keating's column. I was angry and told him to kill the column. Then I called the woman who had given Tom a copy of the poll and told her I should fire her. But being a prudent and compassionate editor, of course, I didn't.

The readers did not know why his column didn't appear, so I got no heat from angry readers, but the staff was outraged. One of the more righteous reporters was even pushing Tom to resign in protest. It was easy for him to make the suggestion. He was single; Tom had a wife and four children.

But I never again killed a local column.

A few years earlier as news editor I had managed to anger our Kokomo readers. The Kokomo High School basketball team had just won the state basketball tournament by defeating Indianapolis's Manual High School in overtime 68-66 at what is now Hinkle Fieldhouse on March 18, 1961. The coveted Trester Award for mental attitude was presented for the first time to twins, Tom and Dick VanArsdale of Manual.

Kokomo fans had no argument with that selection. It was my placing a photo of the twins on the front page of the state edition, the edition that went to Kokomo, that riled them. Where was the Kokomo team's picture? Traditionally, we used a stock photo of the winning team on page one of the state edition, and replaced it with a photo of the team taken after the players had cut down the nets and hung on each other for the victory photo. That victory photo of the Kokomo team made page one in the city edition, but the Kokomo readers assumed that the photo of the twins was on the front page in all of the editions.

The sports editor of the *Kokomo Tribune* went ballistic, declaring that *The Star* had always hated Kokomo. The only thing Indianapolis hated about Kokomo was the traffic jams on the U. S. 31 bypass on the city's outskirts.

I was able to weather the ire of readers and learn from their outbursts. In a sense their anger told me that the readers felt that we had tampered with their paper.

As my 65th birthday neared, I decided it was time to hang it up. The love of gathering and reporting news was being replaced with too many meetings, too many budget sessions. And I began to feel that the new technology with its arcane language was rushing by me. So I retired in 1990. And the staff sent me off with a retirement party at the Press Club that sportswriter Robin Miller enlivened as master of ceremonies. The party gave me an opportunity to hug Susan Bayh, the beautiful wife of Governor Evan Bayh, not once but twice, and it allowed me to give the females on the staff the hugs that were prohibited just a few days earlier.

And as the ancient saying goes, time heals all wounds. One of the gifts I received at the party was one of the Doonesbury strips that caused the uproar 10 years earlier. It was signed: "For Bo Connor—With appreciation and good luck from Garry Trudeau. Aug 31 '90."

— 30 —

About the author . . . .

Lawrence S. (Bo) Connor began his forty-one-year career at *The Star* in 1949 as a police reporter and retired in 1990 as managing editor. He worked in nearly every editorial position on the paper, including a three-month stint as editor of the editorial page. He served three years in the Army Air Corps during World War II and began work at *The Star* after graduating from the University of Notre Dame in 1949. He and his wife, Patty, are the parents of six children and grandparents of 15. They live in Indianapolis. This is Connor's second book. *Hampton Court, Growing up Catholic in Indianapolis between the Wars* was published in 1994 by Guild Press of Indiana.